MEDICAID FINANCIAL ELIG
FOR NURSING HOME CARE
IN NEW YORK STATE

by
Nancy E. Kline

BROOME COUNTY BAR ASSOCIATION

This book was written to provide general, useful information regarding its subject matter. The publisher does not give legal advice. Any reader who needs advice about a specific situation should consult with an attorney.

ISBN-13: 978-0615493459

ISBN-10: 0615493459

Published by the Broome County Bar Association
53 Chenango Street, 2nd Floor, Suite 201, Binghamton NY 13901
Telephone 607-723-6331
www.bcbar.org

ABOUT THE AUTHOR

Nancy E. Kline has been practicing law in upstate New York for over fifteen years. Her practice focuses on the area of elder law, including Wills, Trusts, Estates, Powers of Attorney, Health Care Proxies, and advising people about paying for nursing home care. She lectures at Continuing Legal Education programs for lawyers run by the New York State Bar Association and the Broome County Bar Association. She also speaks at programs for the general public.

She received her undergraduate degree from Yale University, and her law degree from Boston University. She served as Publications Editor of the National College of Probate Judges and Boston University School of Law's Probate Law Journal. She is the author of "Totten Trusts: Dilemmas, Concerns and Suggested Solutions," 9 National College of Probate Judges and Boston University School of Law Probate Law Journal, 117, 1989. She is a member of the Broome County Bar Association, the New York State Bar Association and the National Academy of Elder Law Attorneys.

She is Of Counsel with the law firm Coughlin & Gerhart, L.L.P. in Endicott, New York. She can be reached at P.O. Box 40, Binghamton, NY 13903 or by e-mail at NancyEKline@gmail.com.

TABLE OF CONTENTS

INTRODUCTION

Medicaid will pay the nursing home bills for people who qualify. But who qualifies?

There are several requirements. One big hurdle to Medicaid qualification is financial eligibility. If someone is "too rich," he or she will not qualify for Medicaid. However, merely knowing the total value of someone's assets is not enough to determine whether that person will qualify for Medicaid, because all assets are not treated the same.

Each state has its own financial eligibility rules. This book will discuss the rules for New York State only.

In New York, people are classified by categories, and each category has its own rules. Furthermore, the rules are different based on whether the person is in a nursing home or getting long-term care at home.

This book will focus specifically on the financial eligibility rules for people who are age sixty-five and over who apply to have Medicaid pay their nursing home bills in New York State.

There are other Medicaid eligibility requirements, but they will not be discussed here.

The goal of this book is to provide attorneys with easy access to the citations which will lead them to the financial eligibility rules.

MEDICAID CATEGORIES

Medicaid is a program which assists low income people in getting and paying for medical care. Medicaid Reference Guide, at glossary xii. *

Medicaid is administered by local Departments of Social Services. Medicaid Reference Guide, at glossary xii.

People who apply for Medicaid are divided into categories. The rules are different for each category. An applicant is financially eligible for Medicaid if his net available income and resources are below the standards for his particular category. 18 NYCRR 360-4.8(a)(1).

People who are age sixty-five and over, certified blind or certified disabled are categorized as "SSI-related." N.Y. Social Services Law section 366 (1)(a)(5); 18 NYCRR 360-3.3(b); Medicaid Reference Guide, at 24 and glossary xxi.

"Blind" is defined as the total lack of vision, or residual vision being no better than 20/200 in both eyes with best correction, or restriction of the visual fields, or other factors which affect the usefulness of vision as prescribed in the appropriate medical criteria published by the department. 18 NYCRR 360-5.2(a).

"Disability" is the inability to engage in any substantial gainful activity by reason of any medically determinable physical or mental impairment which can be expected to result in death or has lasted or can be expected to last for a continuous period of not less than twelve months. 18 NYCRR 360-5.2(b).

* The Medicaid Reference Guide was renumbered in January 2011. Citations in this book refer to the new page numbers.

SPOUSE'S RESPONSIBILITY

If the applicant is married, it is important to understand the spouse's rights and responsibilities under the Medicaid financial eligibility rules.

"Spouse" is defined as a person married to a Medicaid applicant/recipient. This includes married people who are separated but not divorced. It does not include people in a common law relationship who are not married. Medicaid Reference Guide, at glossary xxi.

"Community spouse" is defined as a person who is the spouse of an institutionalized person and who is residing in the community. N.Y. Social Services Law section 366-c (1)(b); 18 NYCRR 360-4.10(a)(2). A community spouse is not in a medical institution or nursing facility or receiving services under a Social Security Act section 1915 (c) waiver. N.Y. Social Services Law section 366-c (2)(a) and (b). A community spouse is a person who is the spouse of an institutionalized person, and who is residing in the community and not expected to receive home and community-based services under a Social Security Act section 1915 (c) waiver for at least 30 consecutive days. Medicaid Reference Guide glossary, at iv.

"Institutionalized spouse" is defined as a person in a medical institution or nursing facility who is expected to remain there for at least thirty consecutive days, or who is receiving services or supplies under a Social Security Act section 1915 (c) waiver, and who is married to a person who is not in a medical institution or nursing facility or receiving services under a Social Security Act section 1915 (c) waiver. N.Y. Social Services Law section 366-c (2)(a); 18 NYCRR 360-4.10 (a)(7); 42 U.S.C. section 1396r-5 (h). Medicaid Reference Guide, at glossary xi, adds a 30 day requirement for the waiver portion of the definition.

SAME SEX MARRIAGES PERFORMED ELSEWHERE:

Individuals who declare that they have been legally married in a jurisdiction that recognizes and performs same-sex unions must receive full faith, credit and comity as all other legally married persons when Medicaid eligibility is determined. GIS 08 MA/023, at 1. They must receive equal treatment and recognition of the marriage. Medicaid Reference Guide, at 5. Terms such as "husband," "wife," and "spouse" are construed in a manner that encompasses legal same-sex marriages. GIS 08 MA/023, at 1. Issues which will be affected by this include determinations of who is a legally responsible relative, budgeting, transfer of assets, income from trusts, homestead exemptions, burial funds, estates, and liens and recoveries. GIS 08 MA/023, at 1; Medicaid Reference Guide, at 5. See also Medicaid Reference Guide, at glossary xxi.

Additional issues include required signatures on applications, health insurance premium payments and resource exemptions. Medicaid Reference Guide, at 5.

SPOUSE AS LEGALLY RESPONSIBLE RELATIVE:

In general, if the applicant's spouse is not in a nursing home, the applicant's spouse is allowed to keep a certain amount of resources; under the Medicaid rules, the rest of the applicant's spouse's resources must be used to pay the applicant's medical bills.

A spouse is a legally responsible relative. N.Y. Social Services Law section 366 (2)(b)(1); Medicaid Reference Guide, at 550.

A "legally responsible relative" is a person who is legally responsible for the support and care of one or more relatives. For Medicaid purposes, a legally responsible relative is a spouse of a person applying for or receiving Medicaid, or a parent of a child under the age of twenty-one. 18 NYCRR 360-4.1(h); Medicaid Reference Guide, at glossary xi.

The spouse of a person receiving public assistance shall, if of sufficient ability, be responsible for the support of such person. N.Y. Social Services Law section 101 (1).

 A person is not financially responsible for the Medicaid applicant/recipient unless the person is the applicant/recipient's spouse or the parent if the applicant/recipient is under 21. N.Y. Social Services Law section 366 (b)(1).

Note that a child is not responsible for the support of a parent under the statute.

All resources held by either the applicant or the community spouse or both shall be considered available to the applicant, to the extent that they exceed the community spouse resource allowance. N.Y. Social Services Law section 366-c (5)(a).

The Department of Social Services must consider the income and resources of legally responsible relatives. 18 NYCRR 360-2.3(c)(1).

SPOUSAL REFUSAL:

The applicant's spouse can refuse to use her resources and income to pay the applicant's nursing home bill. The applicant's spouse would do this by signing a letter stating that she refuses to make her resources and income available to the applicant. She would give the letter to the Department of Social Services with the applicant's Medicaid application. If all of the requirements are followed, then the applicant's countable resources would be compared to the financial eligibility level for a single person. The resources and income of the applicant's spouse would be ignored when determining if the applicant qualifies for Medicaid. However, the applicant's spouse can be sued for reimbursement of the amount that Medicaid paid the nursing home.

The resources of a legally responsible relative living in the same household are considered available to the applicant unless the legally responsible relative refuses to make them available. Medicaid Reference Guide, at 406 and 551.

If a legally responsible relative has sufficient income and resources to provide medical assistance, as determined by the regulations, but the legally responsible relative refuses to provide the care and assistance, Medicaid shall be given to the applicant. N.Y. Social Services Law section 366 (3)(a); 18 NYCRR 360-4.10(c)(4); 18 NYCRR 360-4.3 (f)(1)(i); 90 INF-19, at page 3 of the attachment; 42 U.S.C. section 1396r-5(c)(3). In this situation, the resources of the legally responsible relative are ignored when determining Medicaid eligibility. Medicaid Reference Guide, at 468.

The applicant must execute an assignment of his right to pursue support from the community spouse, in favor of the social services district and the department, unless he is unable to execute such an assignment due to physical or mental impairment. 18 NYCRR 360-4.10 (c)(4); 89 ADM-47, at 14-15; 42 U.S.C. section 1396r-5(c)(3).

Granting Medicaid in this situation creates an implied contract with the legally responsible relative. N.Y. Social Services Law section 366 (3)(a); 18 NYCRR 360-7.11(b)(iii); 18 NYCRR 360-4.3 (f)(1)(i); Medicaid Reference Guide, at 468, 552 and 555. The cost of care may be recovered from the legally responsible relative. N.Y. Social Services Law section 366 (3)(a); 02 OMM/ADM-3, at 17; 18 NYCRR 360-4.10 (c)(4); Medicaid Reference Guide, at 468, 552 and 555.

The Department of Social Services should, where cost-effective, seek to recover the cost of medical assistance provided, from the refusing spouse's excess income and resources, including any beneficial interest the refusing spouse has in a trust. 92 ADM-45, at 11.

Note that the recovery sought would be for the cost of medical assistance provided. This would be the amount that actually was paid to the nursing home, not the private pay rate which the applicant would have paid the nursing home if the community spouse did not exercise spousal refusal.

The Department of Social Services need not pursue recovery if it is not cost effective to do so, such as when the cost of recovery will be greater than the amount reasonably expected to be collected. 02 OMM/ADM-3, at 20.

When a Medicaid application is filed, the applicant and spouse must give the Department of Social Services copies of documents showing the value of their resources. A community spouse needs to provide these documents to the Department of Social Services even if she is exercising spousal refusal. If the community spouse refuses to provide the Department of Social Services with information about her resources, Medicaid can be denied for the applicant. 18 NYCRR 360-4.10 (c)(3); 90 ADM-29, at 2; 89 ADM-47, at 13; 90 INF-19, at pages 2-3 of the attachment. However, the applicant will not be ineligible for Medicaid if he executes an assignment on behalf of the Department of Social

Services for his right to pursue support from the community spouse, unless the applicant is unable to execute the assignment due to physical or mental impairments, and denying Medicaid would be an undue hardship. 18 NYCRR 360-4.10 (c)(4); 90 ADM-29, at 2-3; 89 ADM-47, at 13-14; 90 INF-19, at page 2 of the attachment; 42 U.S.C. 1396r-5 (c)(3).

Undue hardship means a situation where:
- a community spouse fails or refuses to cooperate in providing necessary information about her resources
- the institutionalized spouse is otherwise eligible for Medicaid
- the institutionalized spouse is unable to obtain appropriate medical care without Medicaid
AND
- the community spouse's whereabouts are unknown
- or the community spouse is incapable of providing the required information due to illness or mental incapacity
- or the community spouse lived apart from the institutionalized spouse immediately prior to the institutionalization
- or due to the action or inaction of the community spouse (other than the failure or refusal to cooperate in providing information about her resources), the applicant will be in need of protection from actual or threatened harm, neglect or hazardous conditions if discharged from an appropriate medical setting.
18 NYCRR 360-4.10 (a)(12); 90 ADM-29, at 3; 90 INF-19, at page 3 of the attachment (although it did not include the last option).

RESOURCE LEVELS

"Resources" are defined as property of all kinds, including real and personal, tangible and intangible. Medicaid Reference Guide, at glossary xix and 308.

The "resource level" is the highest amount of resources that an applicant can have and qualify for Medicaid. Medicaid Reference Guide, at 409.

Some resources do not count when determining if a person is eligible for Medicaid. After these resources are ignored, what remains are the person's "countable resources." The countable resources are compared to the resource level for the appropriate category to determine if the applicant qualifies for Medicaid. Medicaid Reference Guide, at 382.

If the value of the countable resources is greater than the resource level for the applicant's category, the applicant has "excess resources." Medicaid Reference Guide, at 310.

Resources are valued as of the first day of the month for which the applicant is applying for Medicaid. 93 ADM-29, at 13; Medicaid Reference Guide, at 308 and 408.

Medicaid can be authorized retroactively to pay for medical services which were provided during the three months before the application was filed. In order to get Medicaid for a prior month, the applicant must have been eligible in the month that the services were received. 18 NYCRR 360-2.4(c); 03 OMM/ADM-1, at 10; 42 U.S.C. section 1396a(1)(34).

If the applicant requests Medicaid coverage for the three months prior to when the application was filed, the value and availability of his resources are determined as of the first day of the month for each month that he is seeking coverage. Medicaid Reference Guide, at 308 and 409.

RESOURCE LEVEL FOR THE MEDICAID APPLICANT:

The resource level for the Medicaid applicant is $13,800 for the year 2011. GIS 10 MA/026. This is the same as 2009 and 2010.

RESOURCE LEVEL FOR THE COMMUNITY SPOUSE:

To determine how much the community spouse is allowed to have: add up the countable resources of the applicant and the community spouse. Use the value on the date that the applicant went into the nursing home. Divide by two to determine the community spouse's half. 42 U.S.C. section 1396r-5 (c)(1)(A).

After you determine the community spouse's half, there is a minimum and a maximum to the amount that the community spouse is allowed to keep. For 2011, the minimum is $74,820 and the maximum is $109,560. GIS 10 MA/026. This is the same as 2009 and 2010.

If the community spouse's half is $74,820 or less: the community spouse can keep $74,820.

If the community spouse's half is $109,560 or more: the community spouse can keep $109,560.

For further explanation of how the 50% rule works, see GIS 07 MA/025.

The amount that the community spouse is allowed to have is referred to as the "Community Spouse Resource Allowance" (CSRA). N.Y. Social Services Law section 366-c (2)(d); 18 NYCRR 360-4.10(a)(4); GIS 08 MA/035.

If the community spouse's resources are more than the CSRA, they are considered available to the applicant. 18 NYCRR 360-4.10 (c)(2). This will make the applicant "too rich" for Medicaid.

EXEMPT RESOURCES

When determining if someone is financially eligible for Medicaid, some resources are ignored. They are referred to as "exempt."

HOMESTEAD:

A "homestead" is the primary residence of the applicant and/or members of his family. Family members may include the applicant's spouse, minor children, certified blind or certified disabled children, and other dependent relatives. The homestead includes the home, land and integral parts such as a garage and outbuildings. The homestead may be a condominium, cooperative apartment or mobile home. Vacation homes, summer homes and cabins are not homesteads. 18 NYCRR 360-1.4 (f); Medicaid Reference Guide, at 337 and 338.

Land adjoining the homestead is considered part of the homestead if it is not on a separate deed. GIS 06 MA/009.

INTENT TO RETURN HOME:

A homestead is exempt as long as the applicant intends to return home. 18 NYCRR 360-4.7(a)(1)(ii); 03 OMM/ADM-1, at 7; Medicaid Reference Guide, at 337, 400 and 683.

This is based on what the applicant intends. It is not based on what the medical record shows. It is a subjective standard, not an objective standard of expectations. Anna W. v Bane, 863 F. Supp. 125 (W.D. NY 1993).

Intent to return home can be documented by:
- a written statement from a Department of Social Services caseworker that the applicant stated his intent
- If the applicant cannot state his intent at the time of the application: a past statement of intent
- If the applicant cannot state his intent at the time of the application and never stated his intent in the past: a statement from his attorney-in-fact, health care agent, guardian or authorized representative. An authorized representative is the person the applicant designated to

represent him in the application process. 03 OMM/ADM-1, at 7.

FAMILY MEMBERS LIVING IN THE HOME:

A homestead is exempt as long as the applicant's spouse, child under 21, certified blind or certified disabled child, or other dependent relative lives there. 18 NYCRR 360-4.7 (a)(1)(ii).

PLACING A LIEN ON THE HOME:

Even though the homestead is exempt because the applicant intends to return home, a lien may be placed on the property if the applicant is not reasonably expected to return home. The lien will allow the Department of Social Services to recover its costs when the property is sold. N.Y. Social Services Law section 369 (2)(a)(ii); 18 NYCRR 360-7.11(a)(3); 02 OMM/ADM-3, at 6; 03 OMM/ADM-1, at 4; Medicaid Reference Guide, at 400 and 683; 42 U.S.C. section 1396p (a)(1)(B); 42 U.S.C. section 1396p (b)(a)(A).

A person in a nursing home is presumed to be permanently absent unless adequate medical evidence shows that he is expected to return home. 03 OMM/ADM-1, at 4; Medicaid Reference Guide, at glossary xvi.

It will be presumed that a person will not return home if he enters a skilled nursing facility. 18 NYCRR 36.-1.4(k)(1); Medicaid Reference Guide, at glossary xvi. Adequate medical evidence may overcome this presumption. 18 NYCRR 360-1.4 (k).

CIRCUMSTANCES WHEN A LIEN MAY NOT BE PLACED ON THE HOME:

A lien may not be placed on the homestead if one of the following people lives there: the applicant's spouse, the applicant's child under twenty-one, certified blind or certified disabled child, or the applicant's sibling who has an equity interest in the home and who resided there for at least one year immediately before the applicant went into the nursing

home. N.Y. Social Services Law section 369 (2)(a)(ii)(C); 18 NYCRR
360-7.11(a)(3)(ii); 02 OMM/ADM-3, at 6; 03 OMM/ADM-1, at 4; 92
ADM-53, at 5-6 and 12; 42 U.S.C. section 1396p(a)(2); Medicaid
Reference Guide, at 683.

Before imposing a lien on a homestead, the Department of Social
Services is supposed to give the applicant an opportunity to make an
exempt transfer. The applicant usually is given ninety days after
Medicaid eligibility is determined, but a longer period of time may be
allowed if delays are due to circumstances outside the applicant's
control. 02 OMM/ADM-3, at 7; 03 OMM/ADM-1, at 5 and 8; 92 ADM-
53, at 11; Medicaid Reference Guide at 648. Exempt transfers are
discussed elsewhere in this book.

CIRCUMSTANCES WHEN THERE CAN BE NO RECOVERY ON THE LIEN:

If a lien is imposed on the homestead, no recovery may be made on the
lien if a sibling of the applicant lives in the home. The sibling must have
resided in the home for at least one year before the applicant went into
the nursing home, and must have lawfully resided in the home on a
continuous basis since the applicant went into the nursing home. N.Y.
Social Services Law section 369 (2)(b)(iii)(A); 18 NYCRR 360-7.11
(b)(3)(i); 02 OMM/ADM-3, at 7; 92 ADM-53, at 12; 42 U.S.C. section
1396p(b)(2)B)(i). Note that the sibling is not required to have an equity
interest in the home. The applicant cannot be required to sell the home
if the sibling lives there. 91 ADM-53, at 12. If the sibling no longer
resides in the home, the applicant must agree to sell it. 92 ADM-53, at
12.

If a lien is imposed, no recovery may be made on the lien if a child of
the applicant lives in the home. The child must have resided in the
home for at least two years immediately before the person went into the
nursing home, and must have provided care which let the applicant live
at home rather than having to go into a nursing home. The child must
have lawfully resided in the home on a continuous basis since the
applicant went into the nursing home. N.Y. Social Services Law section
369 (2)(b)(iii)(B); 18 NYCRR 360-7.11 (b)(3)(ii); 02 OMM/ADM-3, at 8;
42 U.S.C. section 1396p (b)(2)(B)(ii). The applicant cannot be required

to sell the house if the child lives there. 91 ADM-53, at 12. If the child no longer resides in the home, the applicant must agree to sell it. 92 ADM-53, at 12. The child is referred to as a "Caretaker Child."

Recovery on the lien shall be waived in cases of undue hardship. N.Y. Social Services Law section 369 (5); 42 U.S.C. section 1396p(b)(3)(A).

If a lien is imposed, it must be removed if the applicant goes home. N.Y. Social Services Law section 369 (2)(a)(ii); 92 ADM-53, at 12; 02 OMM/ADM-3, at 7; 42 U.S.C. section 1396p (a)(3).

THE SUBSTANTIAL HOME EQUITY RULE:

Beginning with Medicaid applications filed on or after 01/01/2006, the homestead is not exempt if the applicant has an equity interest in it which exceeds a certain dollar amount. N.Y. Social Services Law section 366 (2)(a)(1)(ii); 06 OMM/ADM-5, at 7; GIS 06 MA/016, at 2; 42 U.S.C. section 1396p (f); Medicaid Reference Guide, at 401.

The limit originally was $750,000. 06 OMM/ADM-5, at 7. N.Y. Social Services Law section 366 (2)(a)(2)(ii) and 42 U.S.C. section 1396p (f) provide that the limit shall be increased beginning with the year 2011. The amount of the increase shall be determined by the Secretary of the federal Department of Health and Human Services based on the percentage increase in the Consumer Price Index for all urban consumers, rounded to the nearest $1,000. If the Secretary does not determine an amount, the Department of Health shall increase the dollar amount based on the increase in the Consumer Price Index.

Effective 01/01/2011, the limit increased from $750,000 to $758,000. GIS 10 MA/025.

The substantial home equity rule does not apply to people who applied for and were determined eligible for long-term care services prior to 01/01/2006 if they have not had a break in Medicaid eligibility. 06 OMM/ADM-5, at 25.

Equity value is fair market value minus legal encumbrances such as liens and mortgages. 06 OMM/ADM-5, at 25; 42 U.S.C. section 1396p (f)(1)(C)(3); Medicaid Reference Guide, at 401.

A reverse mortgage or home equity loan may be used to decrease home equity. N.Y. Social Services Law section 366 (2)(a)(1)(ii); Medicaid Reference Guide, at 402; 42 U.S.C. section 1396p (f)(3).

Applicants cannot use medical bills to reduce excess home equity. 06 OMM/ADM-5, at 24; Medicaid Reference Guide, at 401.

When proving the value of the homestead, the preferred method is an independent appraisal by a licensed real estate appraiser. If that is not practical, the Department of Social Services is supposed to use the listed asking price accompanied by a market analysis or appraisal; if neither is available, the Department of Social Services is supposed to use a full value tax assessment. Medicaid Reference Guide, at 403. The Department of Social Services cannot require the applicant to pay for an appraisal. Medicaid Reference Guide, at 403.

The substantial home equity rule does not apply if one of the following people lives in the home: spouse; applicant's child under twenty-one; applicant's blind or permanently and totally disabled child. N.Y. Social Services Law section 366 (2)(a)(1)(ii); 06 OMM/ADM-5, at 7 and 25; GIS 06 MA/016, at 2; 42 U.S.C. section 1396p (f)(1)(C)(2); Medicaid Reference Guide, at 402.

People who are subject to the substantial home equity rule may claim undue hardship. N.Y. Social Services Law section 366 (2)(a)(1)(i). Undue hardship exists if denying Medicaid coverage would deprive the person of medical care such that his health or life would be endangered, OR deprive him of food, closing, shelter or other necessities of life, AND there is a legal impediment which prevents him from being able to access his equity interest in the property. 06 OMM/ADM-5, at 7 and 25; Medicaid Reference Guide, at 402.

For purposes of the substantial home equity rule, if the home is jointly owned, each owner is presumed to have an equal interest in the property, unless there is evidence to the contrary. 06 OMM/ADM-5, at 24; Medicaid Reference Guide, at 401.

EXPENSES OF HOME OWNERSHIP:

There are certain expenses associated with owning a home, such as property tax, homeowner's insurance, and utilities. As discussed elsewhere in this book, when a person goes on Medicaid, there are rules which limit the amount of income the person is allowed to keep. A person on Medicaid is not allowed to keep extra income to pay the expenses of home ownership. 03 OMM/ADM-1, at 9.

ALL PROPERTY CONTIGUOUS TO THE HOMESTEAD:

Property contiguous to the homestead is exempt. 18 NYCRR 360-4.6(b)(2)(i); Medicaid Reference Guide, at 340.

"Contiguous property is the land adjoining the homestead and the buildings located on such land. To be considered contiguous, the land must adjoin the plot on which the home is located and must not be separated from it by intervening real property owned by others. Property will be considered to adjoin other property if the only intervening real property is an easement or public right-of-way such as a street, road, or utility line." 18 NYCRR 360-4.6(b)(2)(i).

The Medicaid Reference Guide has several different definitions of the term "contiguous property."

Contiguous property is land adjoining the homestead which is not an integral part of the homestead and can be separately liquidated. Medicaid Reference Guide glossary, at iv.

Contiguous property is land adjoining the homestead which is held on a separate deed from the homestead and which can be liquidated separately. GIS 06 MA/009; Medicaid Reference Guide, at 340.

Property adjoins the homestead if the only intervening real property is an easement or public right of way, such as a street, road or utility. GIS 06 MA/009; Medicaid Reference Guide, at 340.

HOUSEHOLD GOODS:

Essential personal property is exempt. N.Y. Social Services Law section 366 (2)(a)(2); 18 NYCRR 360-4.7 (a)(2); Medicaid Reference Guide, at 346 and 384.

Essential personal property includes but is not limited to clothing and personal effects; household furniture, appliances and equipment; and tools and equipment which are necessary for a trade or business. Essential personal property is exempt. 18 NYCRR 360-4.7 (a)(2).

Items which are considered essential personal property include but are not limited to: household furniture; personal effects; household appliances; televisions; radios; stereos, records, CDs and cassette tapes; china and flatware; clothing; jewelry with sentimental value, such as a wedding ring or engagement ring or family heirloom; books; household tools, such as a lawn mower, garden tools, home repair tools; and tools and equipment which are necessary for a trade, occupation or business. Medicaid Reference Guide, at 346.

The major consideration is whether the applicant or members of his household are using the item. Medicaid Reference Guide, at 347.

If the applicant does not intend to return home, and there are no other family members living in the household, household goods and personal effects may be considered available resources. Medicaid Reference Guide, at 347.

If the applicant invested in jewelry or antiques, they are not exempt. Medicaid Reference Guide, at 347.

If a collection, such as stamps, coins or books, are of limited value, they are exempt. If they are valuable, they are treated as available resources and are not exempt. Medicaid Reference Guide, at 347.

Note that the Medicaid application does not ask for the value of household goods.

AUTOMOBILE:

An automobile is exempt, per 18 NYCRR 360-4.7 (a)(2)(iv).

An automobile is exempt as long as the applicant or a member of his household is using it. GIS 98 MA/007; Medicaid Reference Guide, at 348 and 382.

If the automobile is not in use, it loses its exempt status. Medicaid Reference Guide, at 382.

An automobile is exempt regardless of its value. GIS 98 MA/007.

A second automobile may be exempt if there is a medical need for it. GIS 98 MA/007; GIS 05 MA/029, at 1; Medicaid Reference Guide, at 348, 349 and 382.

An automobile that is temporarily inoperable, such as a car which needs repairs, is exempt if it is expected to be used for transportation for the applicant or a member of his household within twelve months after Medicaid eligibility is determined. GIS 05 MA/029.

GIS 98 MA/007 had an old rule about automobiles. It stated that if the automobile was not exempt, meaning that it was not used by the applicant or a member of his family, it was a countable resource, but $5,400 of its current market value was exempt. If the current market value was more than $5,400 the excess was a countable resource. The test was current market value, not equity value. GIS 05 MA/029 states that effective 04/01/2005, if an automobile is not exempt, its full equity value is a countable resource; the $5,400 rule was eliminated.

LIFE INSURANCE POLICIES:

Life insurance policies with a combined face value of $1,500 or less are exempt. 18 NYCRR 360-4.6(b)(2)(ii); GIS 96 MA/044; Medicaid Reference Guide, at 324 and 383.

If a life insurance policy does not fall within that exemption, it is a countable resource if it has a cash surrender value. Medicaid

Reference Guide, at 324. For Medicaid purposes, the value of the life insurance policy is its cash surrender value. Medicaid Reference Guide, at 324. Term insurance policies usually do not have a cash surrender value, but some types of term insurance policies do. Medicaid Reference Guide, at 325.

The cash value of a life insurance policy is the amount which the insurer would pay if the policy were cancelled before death or maturity. Medicaid Reference Guide, at glossary iii.

If the consent of another person is needed to cash in a policy, and that person does not consent, the policy does not count as a resource. Medicaid Reference Guide, at 326.

IRREVOCABLE FUND FOR THE EXCLUSIVE PURPOSE OF FUNERAL AND BURIAL:

An irrevocable fund for the exclusive purpose of funeral and burial is exempt. N.Y. Social Services Law section 209 (6); Medicaid Reference Guide, at 365 and 385; General Business Law section 453 (1)(d).

If any money remains in the account after payment of funeral expenses, that money goes to the Department of Social Services. N.Y. Social Services Law sections 141 (6) and 209 (6).

There is no dollar limit on the goods and services which may be purchased through an irrevocable pre-need funeral arrangement. GIS 96 MA/044, at 2.

Funds shall be placed in an interest-bearing account; accumulated interest is not countable income. N.Y. Social Services Law section 209 (6).

These accounts are for the applicant and "family member." N.Y. Social Services Law sections 141 (6) and 209 (6); N.Y. General Business Law 453 (1)(d).

BURIAL SPACE ITEMS:

Burial space items for the applicant, spouse, and immediate family members are exempt. 91 ADM-19, at 2.

One burial plot or space per household member is exempt. 18 NYCRR 360-4.7(a)(3); Medicaid Reference Guide, at 382.

The community spouse's burial space items are exempt, because burial space items designated for the applicant's immediate family members are exempt. Medicaid Reference Guide, at 366 and 371.

"Burial space" items include gravesites, crypts, vaults, mausoleums, caskets, urns, other repositories which are customarily and traditionally used for the remains of deceased persons, and the cost of opening and closing graves. Medicaid Reference Guide, glossary at ii, 368 and 371.

Perpetual care of the gravesite, headstones and headstone engraving also are considered burial space items. Medicaid Reference Guide, at 368 and 371.

"Immediate family member" is defined as the applicant's spouse, minor children, adult children, stepchildren, brothers, sisters, parents, and the spouses of these people. They do not need to be dependent upon the applicant. They do not need to be living in the same household as the applicant. Medicaid Reference Guide, at 371.

A burial space is not exempt if final payment has not been made. 91 ADM-19, at 3. If final payment has not been made, the money might qualify as a burial fund. 91 ADM-19, at 4.

BURIAL FUNDS:

A burial fund is for non-burial space items.

Non-burial space items include: topical disinfection, custodial care, dressing/casketing, cosmetology, supervision for visitation and/or funeral services, hearse, death notices, flowers, and out-of-town shipping. Medicaid Reference Guide, at 368.

A burial fund is exempt, to the extent allowed under the cash assistance program to which the applicant is most closely related. N.Y. Social Services Law section 366 (2)(a)(3).

A burial fund of up to $1500 is exempt if the funds are separately identifiable and monitored as a burial fund. 18 NYCRR 360-4.6(b)(1)(ii); 91 ADM-19, at 2-3.

The funds do not need to be segregated if there is an impediment due to circumstances beyond the applicant's control, such as a person in a nursing home who is mentally or physically incapacitated and unable to authorize someone to segregate the funds. 91 ADM-19, at 4.

A $1500 burial fund is exempt if the applicant does not have an irrevocable pre-paid account at a funeral parlor, or if the applicant has less than $1500 designated for non-burial space items in the irrevocable pre-paid account at a funeral parlor. GIS 95 MA/044, at 2; Medicaid Reference Guide, at 382.

The burial fund will be made up first of any life insurance policies with a face value of $1,500 or less. 18 NYCRR 360-4.6 (b)(1)(ii); Medicaid Reference Guide, at 369.

If the combined face value of the applicant's life insurance policies is more than $1,500, the cash value of those policies is a countable resource. However, if the applicant has less than $1,500 in a burial fund, he can bring the burial fund up to $1,500 by designating some of the cash value in the life insurance policies for this purpose. The rest of the cash value in the life insurance policies would be a countable resource. If he wants to do this, he will have to provide a written statement that the entire cash value of the life insurance policy is intended for burial expenses. This will get around the requirement that burial funds cannot be comingled with other funds. It will not protect the portion of the cash value that is not used to bring the burial fund up to $1500; that portion of the cash value of the policy is still a countable resource. Medicaid Reference Guide, at 369-70.

The community spouse can have an exempt $1,500 burial fund in addition to the applicant's burial fund. 91 ADM-19, at 2; Medicaid Reference Guide, at 369.

Interest earned on exempt burial funds, and appreciation in the value of an excluded burial arrangement, which will become part of the separately identified burial fund, are disregarded. 18 NYCRR 360-4.6 (a)(2)(xvii).

EQUITY VALUE OF A TRADE OR BUSINESS:

The equity value of a trade or business, including any real property and liquid resources used to operate it, is exempt. 91 ADM-30, at 4; Medicaid Reference Guide, at 351 and 383; 18 NYCRR 360-4.4(d).

Business property includes but is not limited to motor vehicles, machinery, farm equipment, inventories, supplies, tools, equipment, government permits, livestock and produce. 91 ADM-30, at 4; 18 NYCRR 360-4.4(d); Medicaid Reference Guide, at 351.

The property must be in current use, or there must be a reasonable expectation that it will be used to produce income within twelve months after it stopped producing income. If the applicant is disabled, another twelve months might be allowed. Medicaid Reference Guide, at 351.

Liquid business resources must be held in a separate business account and cannot be comingled with personal funds. Medicaid Reference Guide, at 351.

INCOME-PRODUCING PROPERTY USED IN A TRADE OR BUSINESS:

The equity value of income-producing property used in a trade or business is exempt. 18 NYCRR 360-4.4(d)(2)(i); 91 ADM-30, at 2 and 4.

"Income-producing property" includes real property, buildings, liquid business resources, motor vehicles, machinery, livestock, government permits, inventories, tools and equipment which are used in a trade or business or which produce rents as land-use fees. 18 NYCRR 360-4.4 (d).

Page 4 of 91 ADM-30 states that trade or business property includes but is not limited to the necessary capital and operating assets of the business, such as real property, buildings, inventory, equipment, machinery, livestock, motor vehicles, government permits to engage in income-producing activity (such as licenses, permits and tobacco crop allotments), and property used by an employee for work (such as tools, equipment and uniforms.

For more examples of income-producing property used in a trade or business, see 91 ADM-30, Attachment I, page 1.

"Equity value" is defined as current fair market value less any legal encumbrances. Current fair market value accounts for any appreciation or depreciation in equity value. 91 ADM-30, at 2.

Page 10 of 91 ADM-30 tells Departments of Social Services to get the following documentation for property used in a trade or business:
- the business's prior year's tax returns, to determine the validity of the business and earnings. If the tax returns are not available, the latest available return, a certified statement from an accountant, or business receipts and expenses for the past twelve months.
- A signed statement from the applicant which describes the business, its assets, the number of years it has been operating, and the identity of co-owners.
- A signed statement that liquid resources are used in the business.

In order for income-producing property to be exempt, it must be in current use, or have been in use with a reasonable expectation that use will resume within twelve months from when it was last used as income-producing property. 91 ADM-30, at 7. An additional twelve months may be allowed if the property is not in current use due to a disabling condition of the applicant. 91 ADM-30, at 7.

Page 12 of 91 ADM-30 tells Departments of Social Services to get the following documentation for income-producing property which is not in current use:
- a signed statement indicating the date of last use, the reason it is not

in use, and when the applicant expects to resume use.
- If the property has not been in use after twelve months due to a disabling condition: a signed statement indicating the nature of the condition, the date of last use, and when the applicant expects to resume use. Medical evidence is an indication of whether medical improvement is expected, but it is not conclusive of a person's intent and ability to do at least some work. It cannot be the sole factor used to determine if current use can be reasonably expected to resume.

INCOME-PRODUCING REAL PROPERTY NOT USED IN A TRADE OR BUSINESS:

If income-producing real property not used in a trade or business generates rental income, land-use fees or other income, and it produces an annual net return of less than 6% of its equity value, it is an available resource. 18 NYCRR 360-4.4(d)(2)(ii); 91 ADM-30, at 2 and 4; Medicaid Reference Guide, at 342.

Examples of land-use fees include ownership of timber rights, mineral or oil exploration. 91 ADM-30, at 2 and 4.

See 91 ADM-30, Attachment I, pages 1-2 for additional examples of income-producing property not used in a trade or business.

If it produces an annual net return of 6% or more, the first $12,000 in equity value is exempt, and the rest of the equity value is an available resource. 18 NYCRR 360-4.4(d)(2)(ii); 91 ADM-30, at 4; Medicaid Reference Guide, at 342.

If the rate of return is less than 6%, the Department of Social Services must determine if the low rate is due to circumstances beyond the applicant's control. If the rate of return is below 6% due to extraordinary circumstances beyond the applicant's control, such as drought, fire, or illness, the first $12,000 of equity value can be excluded for a twenty-four-month grace period. The grace period begins on the first day of the tax year following the year in which the rate of return dropped below 6%. 91 ADM-30, at 5; Medicaid Reference Guide, at 343.

If the applicant has more than one parcel of income-producing property which is not used in a trade or business: each parcel is subject to the 6% test, but only a maximum equity value of $12,000 can be exempt. 91 ADM-30, at 5; Medicaid Reference Guide, at 343.

The net income is gross income minus expenses allowed by the IRS to produce that income, except for depreciation and personal business deductions. Medicaid Reference Guide, at 343.

If income-producing real property is part of the person's homestead, it is exempt. Medicaid Reference Guide, at 342.

Page 11 of 91 ADM-30 tells Departments of Social Services to get the following documentation for income-producing property not used in a trade or business:
- the tax returns for the prior year. If they are not available, then other appropriate evidence such as the lease agreement.
- a signed statement of the applicant indicating the number of years he owned the property, the identity of any co-owners, and a description of the property.

OTHER INCOME-PRODUCING PROPERTY NOT USED IN A TRADE OR BUSINESS:

All other income-producing property not used in a trade or business is exempt. 18 NYCRR 360-4.4 (d)(2)(iii).

PROPERTY USED TO PRODUCE GOODS & SERVICES FOR PERSONAL USE:

The first $12,000 in equity value of real property and buildings used to produce goods and services for personal use is exempt. The rest of the equity value is an available resource. 18 NYCRR 360-4.4 (d)(3); 91 ADM-30, at 2 and 5; Medicaid Reference Guide, at 345.

Property other than real property and buildings which is used to produce goods and services for personal use is exempt. 18 NYCRR 360-4.4 (d)(3); 91 ADM-30, at 2 and 5.

Page 5 of 91 ADM-30 defines property used to produce goods and services for personal use as including real or personal property necessary to produce personal goods and services, such as equipment for canning fruits and vegetables, woodcutting tools, implements for hunting and fishing, and mechanized equipment for gardening.

See 91 ADM-30, Attachment I, page 2 for additional examples of property used to produce goods and services for personal use.

Page 12 of 91 ADM-30 tells Departments of Social Services to get the following documentation for property used to produce goods and services for personal use:
- a signed statement describing the property and how it is used.
- If it is real property: documentation of current fair market value and any legal encumbrances.
- If it is not real property: a signed statement estimating fair market value and any encumbrances.

PERSECUTION PAYMENTS:

GERMAN:

German persecution payments are exempt if they remain identifiable as such. 18 NYCRR 360-4.6(b)(2)(iv); Medicaid Reference Guide, at 384.

AUSTRIAN:

Payments made by the Austrian Government under paragraphs 500-506 of the Austrian General Social Insurance Act are exempt if they remain identifiable as such. These payments were made to people who suffered a loss, were imprisoned, unemployed or forced to flee Austria between March 1938 and May 1945 for political, religious or ethnic reasons. 18 NYCRR 360-4.6(b)(2)(viii). 92 ADM-32, at 4 and 6; Medicaid Reference Guide, at 384.

NETHERLANDS:

Netherlands reparation payments are exempt if based on Nazi persecution. Medicaid Reference Guide, at 384.

JAPANESE AMERICANS AND ALEUTS:

Benefits received under the Federal Civil Liberties Act of 1988 and the Aleutian and Pribilof Islands Restitution Act are exempt. 18 NYCRR 360-4.6(b)(6); 91 ADM-8, at 3 and 7. Medicaid Reference Guide, at 384.

NATIVE AMERICAN PAYMENTS:

Interests of individual Native Americans in trust or restricted lands from funds appropriated in satisfaction of judgments are exempt. 18 NYCRR 360-4.6(b)(12); Medicaid Reference Guide, at 383. Seneca Nation Settlement Act payments made by the state and federal governments under P.L. 101-53 to the Seneca Nation are exempt. Medicaid Reference Guide, at 383.

ALASKAN NATIVE CLAIMS SETTLEMENT ACT DISTRIBUTIONS:

The following distributions from a native corporation formed under the ANCSA are exempt as income or resources: cash up to $2,000 per person per year; stock; a partnership interest; land or an interest in land; an interest in a settlement trust. Medicaid Reference Guide, at 383-84.

AGENT ORANGE SETTLEMENT FUND PAYMENTS:

Payments from any fund established under the In re Agent Orange product liability litigation settlement are exempt. Payments from court proceedings brought for personal injuries sustained by veterans resulting from exposure to dioxin or phenoxy herbicides in connection with the war in Indochina from 01/01/1962 through 05/07/1975 are exempt. 18 NYCRR 360-4.6(b)(7); 91 ADM-8; Medicaid Reference Guide, at 385.

SELF-SUPPORT PLANS:

If an applicant is certified blind or certified disabled, any remaining countable resources may be set aside for a plan to achieve self-support in accordance with the provisions of 18 NYCRR 360-4.6(a)(2)(xxi). If over age 65, must be receiving SSI payments or aid under the State Plan for the blind or disabled for the month preceding the month of the 65th birthday. 18 NYCRR 360-4.6(b)(3); Medicaid Reference Guide, at 384-85.

PREVENTATIVE HOUSING PAYMENTS:

Preventative Housing Payments are exempt if received under 18 NYCRR 423.4(1). 18 NYCRR 360-4.6(b)(4); Medicaid Reference Guide, at 385.

DISASTER AND EMERGENCY ASSISTANCE:

Federal payments under the Disaster Relief Act of 1974 (P.L. 93-288) as amended by the Disaster Relief and Emergency Assistance Amendments of 1988 (P.L. 100-707) are exempt. Comparable disaster assistance from states, local governments and disaster assistance organizations also are exempt. 18 NYCRR 360-4.6(b)(11); Medicaid Reference Guide, at 382-83.

RADIATION EXPOSURE PAYMENTS:

Payments from Radiation Exposure Compensation Trust Fund for injuries or deaths resulting from exposure to radiation from nuclear testing and uranium mining are exempt. Medicaid Reference Guide, at 385.

STUDENT LOANS:

Student loans received and retained by a graduate or undergraduate student for educational purposes are exempt. Interest accrued is unearned income in the month received. Medicaid Reference Guide, at 385.

BLOOD PLASMA SETTLEMENTS:

Payments to hemophilia patients with HIV from a federal class action settlement with manufacturers of blood plasma products are exempt. Medicaid Reference Guide, at 382.

ENERGY EMPLOYEES:

Energy Employees Occupational Illness Compensation Program payments for diseases suffered due to work in the nuclear weapons industry are exempt. Medicaid Reference Guide, at 383.

RELOCATION ASSISTANCE:

Payments under federal Title II of the Uniform Relocation Assistance and Real Property Acquisition Policies Act of 1970 are exempt. 19 NYCRR 360-4.6(b)(8); Medicaid Reference Guide, at 383.

RESOURCES WHICH ARE EXEMPT FOR A LIMITED PERIOD OF TIME

RETROACTIVE SSI AND SOCIAL SECURITY BENEFITS:

Retroactive SSI and Social Security benefits received between 10/01/1987 and 09/30/1989 are exempt for nine months after received. 18 NYCRR 360-4.6(b)(2)(v); Medicaid Reference Guide, at 388.

Retroactive SSI and Social Security benefits received on or after 10/01/1989 are exempt for six months after receipt. 18 NYCRR 360-4.6(b)(2)(v).

Retroactive SSI and Social Security benefits received on or after 03/02/2004 are exempt for nine months after received. GIS 04 MA/030, at 1.

Railroad Retirement benefits are exempt for six months after received. GIS 96 MA/028.

Note that the Medicaid Reference Guide states nine months for SSI, Social Security and Railroad Retirement benefits. Medicaid Reference Guide, at 388.

RETROACTIVE AID AND ATTENDANCE VETERANS BENEFITS:

Retroactive Veterans benefits for aid and attendance, unusual medical expenses and/or housebound allowances are exempt in the month received and the following month. Medicaid Reference Guide, at 387.

STATE CRIME VICTIMS ASSISTANCE FUND PAYMENTS:

State Crime Victims Assistance Fund payments are exempt for nine months after received. 18 NYCRR 360-4.6(b)(2)(vi); 92 ADM-32, at 3 and 5; Medicaid Reference Guide, at 388.

RELOCATION ASSISTANCE FROM STATE OR LOCAL GOVERNMENT:

Relocation assistance payments are made when the government requires a person to move. The government might need the person's land for a highway, or the person might need to move because toxic waste was discovered on the land. If received on or after 05/01/1991, they are exempt for nine months after received if comparable to assistance provided under Title II of the Uniform Relocation Assistance and Real Property Acquisitions Policies Act of 1970 which is subject to the treatment required by section 216 of that act. 18 NYCRR 360-4.6(b)(vii); 92 ADM-32, at 3; Medicaid Reference Guide, at 388.

FEDERAL EARNED INCOME TAX CREDIT:

Refunds or advance payments of the Federal Earned Income Tax Credit are exempt for the month received and the following month. 18 NYCRR 360-4.6(b)(9); 92 ADM-32, at 4. Medicaid Reference Guide page 387 states exempt in the month received and the following nine months. Page 1 of GIS 04 MA/030 states that if received on or after 03/02/2004, exempt for nine months after received.

EDUCATION-RELATED EXPENSES:

Grants, scholarships, fellowships or gifts used to pay tuition and other education-related fees at any educational, technical or vocational institution are exempt in the month received and the following nine months. GIS 04 MA/030, at 2; Medicaid Reference Guide, at 387.

REAL PROPERTY SALE PROCEEDS:

The proceeds from the sale of real property are exempt for a reasonable period of time, not to exceed six months, while the individual reinvests the proceeds. Medicaid Reference Guide, at 388.

INSURANCE PAYMENTS:

If an insurance payment is for repairing a lost, damaged or stolen resource which was disregarded, the payment is disregarded for nine months after it is received. If the individual has a good reason for not having replaced the resource, an additional nine months can be exempt. Interest from the payments also is exempt. If the individual uses the payment to purchase a countable resource before the nine or eighteen months is up, the value of the resource is countable. Medicaid Reference Guide, at 387.

CASH PAYMENTS FOR MEDICAL SERVICES OR SOCIAL SERVICES:

Certain cash payments that let the individual pay for medical services or social services are exempt in the month received and for nine months after that. Medicaid Reference Guide, at 387.

RESOURCES WHICH RECEIVE SPECIAL TREATMENT

ANNUITIES:

A person usually purchases an annuity by giving a lump sum of money to a bank or an insurance company. The bank or insurance company will then give the person regular payments of income, either for a certain period of time or for life. Some annuities let the person name a remainder beneficiary, who will receive whatever is left in the annuity when the person dies. HCFA Transmittal 64, section 3258.9(B); 96 ADM-8, at 8.

The Medicaid Reference Guide defines an annuity as an investment vehicle whereby an individual establishes a right to receive fixed or periodic payments, either for life or a term of years. Medicaid Reference Guide glossary i.

For Medicaid purposes, an annuity is considered a trust. 96 ADM-8, at 8.

Trust rules are discussed elsewhere in this book. In general, if it can be cancelled and all of the funds taken out, it is a countable resource. It counts when determining if the applicant qualifies for Medicaid. Funding does not create a penalty period. (A penalty period is a length of time during which Medicaid will not pay the nursing home bill even though the applicant is not "too rich." Penalty periods are discussed elsewhere in this book.) See the rules for revocable inter vivos trusts.

If it cannot be cancelled and all of the funds cannot be taken out, it is not a countable resource. It does not count when determining if the applicant qualifies for Medicaid. See the rules for inter vivos trusts. However, there might be a penalty period if certain conditions are not met. Irrevocable inter vivos trusts are subject to penalty periods if certain actions were taken in the sixty months before the Medicaid application was filed.

"Annuities, although usually purchased in order to provide a source of income for retirement, are occasionally used to shelter assets so that individuals purchasing them can become eligible for Medicaid. In order to avoid penalizing annuities validly purchased as part of a retirement plan but to capture those annuities which abusively shelter assets, a determination must be made with regard to the ultimate purpose of the annuity (i.e., whether the purchase of the annuity constitutes a transfer of assets for less than fair market value.) If the expected return on the annuity is commensurate with a reasonable estimate of the life expectancy of the beneficiary, the annuity can be deemed actuarially sound." HCFA transmittal 64, section 3258.9 (B).

There is a penalty period if an annuity is not actuarially sound. HCFA Transmittal 64, section 3258.9(B). An annuity is actuarially sound if the anticipated return on principal and interest does not exceed the person's life expectancy. 06 OMM/ADM-5, at 4. To determine if an annuity is actuarially sound, look at the person's life expectancy. Look at the annuity payment schedule. If the person is not expected to live long enough to receive all the payments from the annuity, the annuity is not actuarially sound. HCFA Transmittal 64, section 3258.9(B).

Example # 1: The annuity will be paid out over 10 years. The person's life expectancy is 14 years. The annuity is actuarially sound. No penalty period.

Example # 2: The annuity will be paid out over 10 years. The person's life expectancy is 8 years. The annuity is not actuarially sound. It will be subject to a penalty period.

When applying for or getting recertified for Medicaid, the applicant must disclose any interest which he or the community spouse has in an annuity. N.Y. Social Services Law section 366-a (10); 06 OMM/ADM-5, at 5 and 22; GIS 06 MA/016, at 1; 42 U.S.C. section 1396p (e)(1); Medicaid Reference Guide, at 452.

If the annuity was purchased after 02/08/2006, the State must be named as remainder beneficiary. N.Y. Social Services Law section 366-a (10); 06 OMM/ADM-5, at 5-6 and 22; GIS MA/016, at 1; Medicaid Reference Guide at 452. If the State is not named as remainder beneficiary, there will be a penalty period. N.Y. Social Services Law section 366 (5)(e)(3)(i); 06 OMM/ADM-5, at 6 and 22; Medicaid Reference Guide, at 457. However, if there is a community spouse or minor or disabled child, they can be the beneficiary, but the

State must be named as the secondary beneficiary. N.Y. Social Services Law section 366 (5)(e)(3)(i); 06 OMM/ADM-5, at 6; 42 U.S.C. section 1396p (c)(1)(F); 42 U.S.C. section 1396p(e); Medicaid Reference Guide, at 452.

If the annuity is a countable resource, the state does not need to be named as Remainder beneficiary. Medicaid Reference Guide, at 452. This is spelled out in part two of the Medicaid application (the Access New York Supplement A).

If the annuity was purchased after 02/08/2006, it must be irrevocable, non-assignable, actuarially sound, provide for payments in equal amounts during the term, and not allow deferral or balloon payments. 06 OMM/ADM-5, at 6 and 23; 42 U.S.C. section 1396p (c)(1)(G)(ii); Medicaid Reference Guide, at 454. If the annuity does not meet these requirements, it is subject to a penalty period. 06 OMM/ADM-5, at 6.

If an annuity was purchased prior to 02/08/06, it will fall within the rules for annuities purchased on or after 02/08/06 if the individual takes actions which change the course of payment from the annuity; changes treatment of income or principal; adds to principal; elects a withdrawal; changes distributions; or annuitizes the annuity. 06 OMM/ADM-5, at 6 and 23; Medicaid Reference Guide, at 454.

The Department of Social Services must be provided with a copy of the annuity contract for an annuity owned by the applicant or the spouse, in order to verify the beneficiary designation. Failure to provide it will result in the annuity being subject to a penalty period. 06 OMM/ADM-5, at 22; Medicaid Reference Guide, at 452.

RETIREMENT FUNDS:

Retirement funds are annuities or work-related plans which provide income when employment ends. Examples of retirement funds are pension, disability, IRAs and Keogh plans. GIS 98 MA/024, at 1; GIS 06 MA/004; Medicaid Reference Guide, at 135 and 316. Some profit-sharing plans may qualify as retirement plans, depending on the requirements established by the employer. Medicaid Reference Guide, at 135 and 316.

Periodic retirement benefits are payments made to an individual at some regular interval (monthly, quarterly, annually), which result from entitlement under a retirement fund. Medicaid Reference Guide, at 135.

A person is eligible for periodic payments if he is able to receive distributions on a regularly scheduled basis without having a penalty. An individual is not entitled to periodic payments if he is not permitted to take regularly scheduled withdrawals penalty free. Ordinary taxes are not considered a penalty. Medicaid Reference Guide, at 135.

MEDICAID APPLICANT'S RETIREMENT FUND:

When determining Medicaid eligibility, the applicant's retirement fund does not count if the applicant is receiving periodic payments from it. GIS 98 MA/024, at 2; Medicaid Reference Guide, at 316.

If a person has a traditional IRA and is older than 70½, the Internal Revenue Code requires him to take Required Minimum Distributions (RMDs) from the IRA each year. See 26 U.S.C. section 408 (a) and 26 U.S.C. section 401 (a)(9). If an applicant is taking RMDs, he is receiving "periodic payments" for Medicaid purposes.

Thus, if the applicant is older than 70½ and has a traditional IRA, the IRA will not count for Medicaid eligibility purposes.

If a Medicaid applicant is eligible for periodic benefits, he must apply for them as a condition of Medicaid eligibility. GIS 98 MA/024, at 2; Medicaid Reference Guide, at 135 and 317.

If a person is under age 70½, the Internal Revenue Code does not require the person to take distributions from a traditional IRA. However, a Medicaid applicant who is younger than 70½ can contact the bank or company where the IRA is held, and arrange to take distributions from the IRA based on life expectancy. These distributions would be "periodic payments" for Medicaid purposes. The IRA would not count when determining Medicaid financial eligibility.

An individual who ordinarily might not be eligible for benefits may be able to access the retirement fund sooner, without incurring a penalty under certain circumstances. Medicaid Reference Guide, at 135.

When determining Medicaid eligibility, a retirement fund counts if the applicant is allowed to withdraw any of the funds but is not entitled to periodic payments. GIS 98 MA/024, at 1; Medicaid Reference Guide, at 316. For Medicaid eligibility purposes, the value of the retirement fund would be the amount that can currently be withdrawn. GIS 98 MA/024, at 1. Penalties for early withdrawal are subtracted when calculating the countable value; income taxes are not subtracted. GIS 98 MA/024, at 1.

SIZE OF DISTRIBUTIONS FROM THE RETIREMENT FUND:

People who have traditional IRAs often want to take out the smallest amount they can. If someone is not applying for Medicaid, he can withdraw the Required Minimum Distribution amount, which is determined by the IRS. However, if someone is applying for Medicaid, and wants his traditional IRA to be ignored for Medicaid financial eligibility purposes, he will have to withdraw the amount required by the Department of Social Services. The Department of Social Services probably will require him to take out more than the IRS's Required Minimum Distribution. Departments of Social Services were requiring that withdrawals be based on the life expectancy table in 96 ADM-8. They may now be requiring that withdrawals be based on the life expectancy table of 06 OMM/ADM-5.

The Medicaid applicant must choose the maximum payment that can be made over the person's lifetime. GIS 98 MA/024, at 2; Medicaid Reference Guide, at 135, 136 and 317.

Example for a Medicaid applicant who was born on 03/21/1923 and has a wife who is 4½ years younger than he is:

To calculate his RMD for IRS purposes, use Table III from Publication 590 Individual Retirement Arrangements. Table III is for married owners whose spouses are not more than 10 years younger. The publication can be found at www.irs.gov.

RMD is calculated based on the balance in the IRA on December 31 of the prior year.

On 12/31/2009, the balance in his IRA was $17,142.32
In 2010 he turned 87.
Table III states that if he is age 87, he has a 13.4 year distribution period.
$17,142.32 ÷ 13.4 = a RMD of $1,279.28 must be taken during the year 2010.

Attachment IV of 96 ADM-8 states that the life expectancy of an 87-year-old male is 4.61 years.
$17,142.32 ÷ 4.61 = a distribution of $3,718.51 to take during the year 2010.

Attachment VIII of 06 OMM/ADM-5 states that the life expectancy of an 87-year-old male is 4.56 years.
$17,142.32 ÷ 4.56 = a distribution of $3,759.28 to take during the year 2010.

If he were not applying for Medicaid, he would have withdrawn the RMD amount during 2010, which is $1,279.28. But if he were applying for Medicaid, and he wanted his IRA to be ignored when determining his Medicaid financial eligibility, the Department of Social Services probably would have required him to withdraw the amount based on 06 OMM/ADM-5 during 2010, which is $3,759.28.

COMMUNITY SPOUSE'S RETIREMENT FUND:

If the community spouse has a traditional IRA, it is not a countable resource. 18 NYCRR 360-4.6(b)(2)(iii).

Page 136 of the Medicaid Reference Guide states that the community spouse does not have to apply for periodic payments or maximize income from a retirement fund.

Page 1 of GIS 98 MA/024 states that a community spouse's retirement funds are countable when determining the total combined countable resources of the couple. They are not considered available to the applicant. They are counted first toward the maximum Community Spouse Resource Allowance.

GIS 06 MA/004 states that a community spouse's retirement fund had been counted first toward the Community Spouse Resource Allowance, and any amount over the Community Spouse Resource Allowance was disregarded. This GIS states that the policy changed, and the excess will no longer be disregarded. If the community spouse is not receiving periodic payments from a retirement fund, it is a countable resource when calculating the Community Spouse Resource Allowance and the institutionalized spouse's Medicaid eligibility. However, if the community spouse is receiving period payments from the retirement fund, it is not counted when determining the institutionalized spouse's eligibility. See also Medicaid Reference Guide, at 257-258 and 333.

GIS 06 MA/004 also states that when determining Medicaid eligibility for SSI-related individuals who are not subject to spousal impoverishment budgeting, a retirement fund owned by a non-applying or ineligible spouse continues to be excluded as a resource.

TREATMENT OF THE DISTRIBUTIONS:

If a person is receiving periodic payments from a retirement fund, they are treated as unearned income. GIS 98 MA/024, at 2; Medicaid Reference Guide, at 135. If the periodic payment is received once a year, it is divided by 12 to arrive at a monthly income amount. GIS 98 MA/024, at 2. The Medicaid income rules are discussed elsewhere in this book.

ROTH IRAS:

The Internal Revenue Code does not require a person to take Required Minimum Distributions from a Roth IRA. However, distributions can be taken from a Roth IRA. If the Medicaid applicant or the community spouse has a Roth IRA and begins taking distributions from it, the Roth IRA might be treated as an exempt resource for Medicaid financial eligibility purposes.

LIFE ESTATES:

A life estate is a limited interest in real property. Medicaid Reference Guide, glossary xi and 353.

The holder of a life estate does not have full title to the property; the holder of a life estate has the right to use the property during his lifetime. 96 ADM-8, at 19; Medicaid Reference Guide, at 353.

When determining Medicaid eligibility, a life estate does not count as a resource. 96 ADM-8, at 21; 03 OMM/ADM-1, at 5; Medicaid Reference Guide, at 353.

Since life estates are not countable resources, the Department of Social Services cannot require the Medicaid applicant/recipient to try to liquidate his life estate. 96 ADM-8, at 21; Medicaid Reference Guide, at 353.

Since life estates are not countable resources, the Department of Social Services cannot require the Medicaid applicant/recipient to try to rent his life estate property. 96 ADM-8, at 21; Medicaid Reference Guide, at 353.

If the property is rented, it is the life estate (not the remainder interest) which is being rented. For Medicaid purposes, the net rental income is countable income for the holder of the life estate. 96 ADM-8, at 21; Medicaid Reference Guide, at 353. It is assumed that the life estate holder pays taxes and maintenance on the property, unless the deed says otherwise. These costs can be deducted from the rental income. 96 ADM-8, at 21; Medicaid Reference Guide, at 354. The Medicaid income rules are discussed elsewhere in this book.

No lien may be placed on a life estate. 96 ADM-8, at 21; 03 OMM/ADM-1, at 5; Medicaid Reference Guide, at 353.

A life tenant usually can receive the same property tax breaks as an owner. See New York State Office of Real Property Service Opinions of Counsel, vol. 3, no. 45 for veterans and senior citizens exemptions. This can be found at www.orps.state.ny.us/legal. Click on Opinions of Counsel. The Office of Real Property Services website states that a life tenant can get the STAR exemption.

LIFE ESTATES AND PENALTY PERIODS:

Medicaid sometimes imposes penalty periods if assets are transferred for less than fair market value. These rules are discussed elsewhere in this book. However, there are some penalty period rules specifically for life estates.

If a Medicaid applicant transferred property for less than fair market value during the look-back period and retained a life estate: if there will be a penalty period, subtract the value of the life estate from the fair market value of the property when determining the amount on which the penalty period will be based. 96 ADM-8, at 20; Medicaid Reference Guide, at 353.

If a person transfers property while retaining a life estate, the value of a life estate is evaluated using a reasonable method of calculating value, based on the current fair market value of the property and the age of the person. 96 ADM-8, at 19; Medicaid Reference Guide, at 353. Social Service Districts may, but are not required to, use the life estate and remainder interest table attached to 96 ADM-8 when calculating the value of life estates and remainder interests. 96 ADM-8, at 20; Medicaid Reference Guide, at 353.

If a Medicaid applicant had a life estate, and transferred that life estate for less than fair market value during the look-back period: there will be a penalty period, unless it is an exempt transfer. 96 ADM-8, at 20-21.

If the property is sold, the life estate is sold and the remainder interest is sold. The proceeds from the sale of the life estate are a countable resource for the person who held the life estate. 96 ADM-8, at 21; Medicaid Reference Guide, at 353. If the person holding the life estate does not take the proceeds from the sale of the life estate, he has made a transfer of assets for less than fair market value. A penalty period will be calculated. 96 ADM-8, at 21.

LIFE INSURANCE POLICIES ISSUED BY PRUDENTIAL OR METLIFE:

On 12/18/2001, Prudential "demutualized." They distributed shares of Prudential Financial common stock to people who had life insurance policies with Prudential. Stock certificates were not issued; the stock was held in book entry form. At the time of the distribution, some people chose to receive cash compensation rather than taking the stock. Many of the rest have no idea that they own Prudential stock. To determine if someone owns Prudential stock from the demutualization, call 800-243-1701. They can search by Social Security Number or by the life insurance policy number. In April 2000, MetLife did the same thing. To determine if someone owns MetLife stock from the demutualization, call 800-649-3593. The Departments of Social Services are aware of these demutualizations. If an application is filed and the applicant has a life insurance policy from Prudential or MetLife, DSS will ask if the person owns the stock.

CONTINUING CARE RETIREMENT COMMUNITY CONTRACTS:

For Medicaid applications filed on or after 08/01/2006, entrance fees in a continuing care retirement community are a resource if the person can use the entrance fee to pay for care; the person is eligible for a refund when he dies or leaves; and the fee does not give him an ownership interest in the CCRC. 06 OMM/ADM-5, at 26; 42 U.S.C. section 1396p (g); Medicaid Reference Guide, at 404.

ASSETS WITH A LEGAL IMPEDIMENT PREVENTING SALE:

When determining Medicaid eligibility, a resource does not count if it cannot be liquidated due to a legal impediment. 03 OMM/ADM-1, at 10; Medicaid Reference Guide, at 500.

A legal impediment exists when the applicant needs a co-owner's consent to sell a jointly owned asset, and the co-owner refuses to sell. 03 OMM/ADM-1, at 10

If a resource cannot be sold due to a legal impediment, a lien must be imposed on the applicant's interest in it, unless it is the applicant's former primary residence and it is occupied by a sibling with equity interest who has resided there for at least one year prior to the A/R's admission into the nursing home. 03 OMM/ADM-1, at 10.

JOINT ASSETS:

The Medicaid eligibility rules for joint accounts depend on whether or not the account is held in a financial institution.

JOINT ACCOUNTS IN FINANCIAL INSTITUTIONS:

Financial institution accounts include savings, checking, time deposits and certificates of deposit. 96 ADM-8, at 18. Page 311 of the Medicaid Reference Guide also includes money market accounts in the definition. For a discussion of whether an asset is a "financial institution account," see In re FH, fair hearing # 3295672N, March 8, 2000.

It is presumed that all of the funds in a financial institution account belong to the Medicaid applicant. 96 ADM-8, at 18; Medicaid Reference Guide at 500. Note that page 253 of the Medicaid Reference Guide specifies "savings account" in a financial institution.

The presumption can be rebutted. Medicaid Reference Guide, at 312. The owners must be given the opportunity to rebut the presumption of ownership and show that the funds did not belong to the Medicaid applicant. HCFA Transmittal 64, section 3258.7.

To rebut the presumptions, the Medicaid applicant must:
- submit a written statement along with corroborating written statements from other account holders, regarding who owns the funds, why there is a joint account, who has made deposits and withdrawals, and how withdrawals have been spent AND
- submit account records for the months for which ownership of the funds is at issue AND
- separate the funds owned by the applicant from the funds of the other account owners. 96 ADM-8, at 18-19.

OTHER JOINT ACCOUNTS:

If a joint asset is not a financial institution account, it is presumed that all joint owners own equal shares, unless there is documentation to the contrary. 96 ADM-8, at 18; Medicaid Reference Guide, at 500.

ADDING A JOINT OWNER: TRANSFER OF ASSETS?

Sometimes, adding a joint owner to an asset is treated as a transfer of assets for less than fair market value, which would be subject to a penalty period.

Merely adding another person's name to an account as a joint owner does not necessarily constitute a transfer of assets. 96 ADM-8, at 19; HCFA Transmittal 64, section 3258.7. The original owner might still have ownership rights to the asset, and have the right to withdraw all of the funds in the account at any time. 96 ADM-8, at 19; HCFA Transmittal 64, section 3258.7

If adding another person's name to the account or asset limits the original owner's right to sell or otherwise dispose of the asset, then adding the name constitutes a transfer of assets. 96 ADM-8, at 19; HCFA Transmittal 64, section 3258.7.

For example, if adding another person's name means that selling the asset would require the new person to agree, then adding the name is a transfer of assets. 96 ADM-8, at 19; HCFA Transmittal 64, section 3258.7.

OTHER ACTIONS: TRANSFER OF ASSETS?

If an account is jointly owned, the asset is considered transferred by the Medicaid applicant when any action is taken, either by him or by the other owner, which reduces or eliminates his ownership or control of the asset. See N.Y. Social Services Law section 366 (5)(d)(5) for actions taken between 08/11/1993 and 02/07/2006. See N.Y. Social Services Law section 366 (5)(e)(6) for actions taken on or after 02/08/2006. See also 18 NYCRR 360-4.4 (c)(2)(vi); 96 ADM-8, at 19; 42 U.S.C. section

1396p (c)(3); HCFA Transmittal 64, section 3258.7.

If the other owner withdraws funds from the account or removes the asset, then the funds or asset are out of the control of the Medicaid applicant; this constitutes a transfer of assets. 96 ADM-8, at 19; HCFA Transmittal 64, section 3258.7.

LIENS AND JOINT ASSETS:

A lien may be imposed on a home owned jointly by the Medicaid applicant and another person, subject to the limitations set forth in IV-E-3. 92 ADM-53, at 13. When the property is liquidated, the Medicaid applicant/recipient's portion of the proceeds of the liquidation are subject to the lien. 92 ADM-53, at 13. The limitations in IV-E-3 of this ADM are that DSS cannot impose a lien on the home of an institutionalized individual as long as one of the following relatives lawfully resides in the home on a continuing basis: spouse; minor child, or child who is certified blind or certified disabled; or sibling with an equity interest in the home who was residing in the home for at least one year. 92 ADM-53, at 12.

JOINT ASSETS AND LEGAL IMPEDIMENTS:

If a resource is jointly owned, and the joint owner's consent is needed to sell the resource, a legal impediment exists if the joint owner refuses to consent to the sale. 03 OMM/ADM-1, at 10; Medicaid Reference Guide, at 500.

BANK ACCOUNTS WITH NAMED BENEFICIARIES:

If a bank account has a named beneficiary, it is owned ITF (in trust for) the beneficiary. When the owner dies, any funds remaining in the account will be paid to the beneficiary. The beneficiary has no ownership interest in the account while the owner is alive. For Medicaid purposes, the entire account belongs to the owner, and none of the account belongs to the beneficiary. Medicaid Reference Guide, at 311.

U.S. SAVINGS BONDS:

Some U.S. savings bonds must be held for a minimum period of time before they can be cashed in. GIS 08 MA/006, at 1. Generally, these bonds are not considered an available resource until after the minimum retention period has expired. GIS 08 MA/006, at 1; Medicaid Reference Guide, at 328.

Series EE bonds issued on or before 01/01/2003 have a minimum retention period of six months. GIS 08 MA/006, at 1; 31 C.F.R. section 351.6 (a).

Series EE bonds issued on or after 02/01/2003 have a minimum retention period of twelve months. GIS 08 MA/006, at 1; 31 C.F.R. section 351.6 (b).

Series I bonds issued on or before 01/01/2003 have a minimum retention period of six months. GIS 08 MA/006, at 1; 31 C.F.R. section 360.35 (b).

Series I bonds issued on or after 02/01/2003 have a minimum retention period of twelve months. GIS 08 MA/006, at 1; 31 C.F.R. section 360.35 (b).

The minimum retention period can be waived in cases of undue hardship. GIS 08 MA/006, at 1. See C.F.R. section 351.85 for Series EE bonds and 31 C.F.R. section 360.90 for Series I bonds. Undue hardship includes unusual or excessive medical expenses. GIS 08 MA/006, at 1; Medicaid Reference Guide, at 329. If someone is applying for Medicaid to pay for nursing home care, he is likely to fall under the undue hardship rule. GIS 08 MA/006, at 1.

As a condition of Medicaid eligibility, the applicant must ask the U.S. Department of the Treasury to waive the minimum retention period. GIS 08 MA/006, at 1; Medicaid Reference Guide, at 328. He must file a copy of the request with DSS. GIS 08 MA/006, at 2; Medicaid Reference Guide, at 329. If he fails to cooperate, his Medicaid application can be denied. GIS 08 MA/006, at 2.

While waiting for a decision on the savings bond undue hardship waiver, the bond is not treated as an available resource for Medicaid eligibility purposes. GIS 08 MA/006, at 2; Medicaid Reference Guide, at 329.

If the savings bond undue hardship waiver is approved, the bond is treated as an available resource as of the first day of the month after the bond is available. GIS 08 MA/006, at 2; Medicaid Reference Guide, at 329. When the bond is cashed in, there may be a penalty withheld from the proceeds; the available amount is the amount actually received. GIS 08 MA/006, at 2; Medicaid Reference Guide, at 329. Income tax due on the proceeds is not an allowable deduction when determining the value of the bond for Medicaid purposes. GIS 08 MA/006, at 2; Medicaid Reference Guide, at 329.

If the savings bond undue hardship waiver is denied, the bond is not treated as an available resource until the minimum retention period ends. GIS 08 MA/006, at 2; Medicaid Reference Guide, at 329. If the waiver is denied, the applicant must file a copy of the denial with DSS. GIS 08 MA/006, at 2; Medicaid Reference Guide, at 330.

If a person other than the Medicaid applicant will not relinquish the bond, the bond is not considered an available resource. Medicaid Reference Guide, at 330.

EXCESS RESOURCES & MEDICAL BILLS

If the applicant would be "too rich" for Medicaid, medical bills can be deducted from the excess resources. 06 OMM/ADM-5, at 12. If qualifying medical bills are more than the excess resources, the applicant will be eligible for Medicaid. 06 OMM/ADM-5, at 12; 91 ADM-17, at 3; Medicaid Reference Guide, at 408 and 410.

The applicant will have to pay those bills. Thus, when doing the calculation to determine when the applicant will qualify, do not include the nursing home bill for the month for which the applicant wants coverage, because the applicant would have to pay that bill.

When medical bills are equal to or greater than the amount of excess resources, the excess resource amount becomes the client's liability. 91 ADM-17, at 6;   Medicaid Reference Guide, at 410.

A Medicaid applicant whose net available resources exceed the resource standard will be ineligible for Medicaid until he incurs medical expenses equal to or greater than the excess resources. 18 NYCRR 360-4.8 (b); 18 NYCRR 360-4.1 (b)(1)(v); 91 ADM-17, at 2.

"Incurred bills" are medical bills received for any date of service that are not covered by third-party health insurance. 91 ADM-17, at 3.

A viable bill may be used in more than one month to offset excess resources and establish eligibility. 91 ADM-17, at 4.

A "viable bill" is an unpaid medical bill where the provider is still seeking payment. 91 ADM-17, at 3.

Medical bills paid by public programs will be used to reduce excess resources and will be considered viable for a maximum of 6 consecutive months from the month Medicaid coverage is first sought. 91 ADM-17, at 4.

Medical bills used to offset excess resources are those owed as of the first of the month, bills for medical services provided during that month, and bills paid during that month. 91 ADM-17, at Attachment III.

Medicaid Reference Guide, at 409, has the procedure for determining when the applicant will qualify for Medicaid:

Step 1: Determine the value of the applicant's resources as of the first day of the month for which he is seeking coverage. If he is seeking coverage for bills during the three-month retroactive period, determine the value of his resources as of the first day of the month for each retroactive month that he is seeking coverage.

Step 2: Determine whether an irrevocable pre-need funeral agreement exists.

Step 3: Determine the amount of his medical bills. Bills are applied against excess resources in the following order:
a) "Viable bills" as of the first of the month.
b) Viable bills for medical expenses incurred during the month.
c) Bills paid by the applicant during the month.
d) Bills paid by public programs.
See also 91 ADM-17, at 6 for Step 3.

91 ADM-17 has an example on pages 1-2 of Attachment I:
Applicant applies on August 5.
She already has burial space items and a $1500 burial fund.
The three-month retroactive period would be July, June and May.

Medical bills:

04/25	$500
05/30	$300
06/04 – 06/15	$8,000
06/20	$200
07/05	$100

Eligibility for May:

Resources as of 05/01		5,000
Resource level	-	3,000
Excess resources		2,000
Bills	-	500
	-	300
		1,200 Is she eligible for May? No.

48

Eligibility for June:

Resources as of 06/01		5,500
Resource level	-	3,000
Excess resources		2,500
Bills	-	500
	-	300
	-	8,000
	-	200
		(6,500) Is she eligible for June? Yes.

Eligibility for July:

Resources as of 07/01		5,200
Resource level	-	3,000
Excess resources		2,200

They have already considered an excess of more than $2,200.
She does not have more resources than she did on June 1.
She is fully eligible for July.

Eligibility for August:

Resources as of 08/01		5,200
Resource level	-	3,000
Excess resources		2,200

They have already considered an excess of more than $2,200.
She does not have more resources than she did on June 1.
She is fully eligible for August.

EXCESS RESOURCES AND FUNERAL AND BURIAL EXPENSES

If you have not filed a Medicaid application because you think the applicant (and his spouse, if applicable) would be "too rich," make sure that the applicant has an irrevocable fund for the exclusive purpose of funeral and burial. Also make sure all burial space items have been purchased for the applicant. In addition, make sure all burial space items have been purchased for the community spouse, and that the community spouse has a $1500 burial fund. These things can be paid to bring the applicant and his spouse under the Medicaid resource levels.

Excess resources may be spent on an irrevocable pre-need funeral agreement. 06 OMM/ADM-5, at 12. An applicant will be given 10 days from the date he is advised of excess resources to reduce those excess resources by establishing a burial fund. 91 ADM-17, at 4 and 6. An applicant will be advised that he also may spend excess resources on exempt burial space items during the 10-day period. 91 ADM-17, at 4 and 6.

Irrevocable funds for the exclusive purpose of funeral and burial expenses, burial space items and burial funds are discussed in detail under Exempt Resources.

TRANSFERS OF ASSETS

Even if the applicant and spouse are not too rich for Medicaid, Medicaid will not pay the applicant's nursing home bill if the applicant or spouse made transfers and received less than fair market value during a certain time period.

The Access NY Supplement A portion of the Medicaid application asks, "Did you, your spouse, or someone on your behalf transfer, change ownership in, give away, or sell any assets, including your home or other real property?"

THE LOOK-BACK PERIOD:

The Department of Social Services does not need information about any transfer or sale ever made. DSS is only looking for transfers and sales made during a certain time frame. This time frame is called "the look-back period." Social Services Law section 366 (5)(d)(1)(vi); 18 NYCRR 360-4.4 (c)(2)(i)(c); 42 U.S.C. section 1396p (c)(1)(B).

The look-back period was thirty-six months. The Federal Deficit Reduction Act of 2005 changed that. It stated that for transfers made on or after 02/08/06, the look-back date would be sixty months. 42 U.S.C. section 1396p(c)(1)(B.

The New York State legislature passed a statute which stated that for transfers made on or after 02/08/06, "look-back period" means the sixty-month period immediately preceding the date that an institutionalized individual is both institutionalized and has applied for Medicaid. N.Y. Social Services Law section 366 (5)(e)(1)(vi).

However, the New York State Department of Health decided that the sixty-month time frame would be phased in. It issued an Administrative Directive to the Commissioners of Social Services which stated that social service districts "will continue to request resource documentation for the past 36 months (60 months for trusts) until February 1, 2009. Beginning February 1, 2009, districts will require resource documentation for the past 37 months (60 months for trusts). The look-back period will increase by one-month increments until February,

2011. Effective February 1, 2011, the full 60-month look-back period will be in place for all transfers of assets." 06 OMM/ADM 5, at 11.

At this time, the sixty-month look-back period is in effect.

THE PENALTY PERIOD:

If the applicant or the spouse made a transfer for less than fair market value during the look-back period, Medicaid will not pay the nursing home bill for a certain period of time. 42 U.S.C. section 1396p (c)(1)(A). This is called the "penalty period." 96 ADM-8, at 15; Medicaid Reference Guide, at 441. For transfers made between 08/11/1993 and 02/07/2006, see N.Y. Social Services Law section 366 (5)(d)(3). For transfers made on or after 02/08/2006, see N.Y. Social Services Law section 366 (5)(e)(3). See also 18 NYCRR 360-4.4 (c)(2)(iii).

When filing a Medicaid application, the applicant and spouse must provide documentation such as bank statements, credit union statements, and brokerage account statements, going back for the length of the look-back period. The Department of Social Services will look through these documents to check for transfers made during the look-back period. 18 NYCRR 360-2.3(c)(3).

Page 2 of the Access NY Supplement A part of the Medicaid application states, "On a separate sheet of paper, provide an explanation of each transaction of $2,000 or more. Medicaid retains the right to review all transactions made during the transfer look-back period."

Page 9 of 10 OHIP/INF-1 states that the $2,000 amount was chosen as a set dollar amount for bank transactions statewide. Each Department of Social Services has discretion on a case-by-case basis to request explanations for transactions of less than $2,000.

If the Department of Social Services identifies transfers for less than fair market value, they can review all transactions made during the look-back period. 10 OHIP/ADM-5, at 12-13.

"Assets" include all income and resources of the applicant and the spouse, including income or resources to which the applicant or the spouse is entitled but which are not received because of action or inaction by: the applicant or the applicant's spouse; a person with legal authority to act in place of or on behalf of the applicant or the spouse; a person acting at the direction or upon the request of the applicant or the spouse; a court or administrative body with legal authority to act in place of or on behalf of the applicant or the spouse or at the direction or upon the request of the applicant or the spouse. N.Y. See Social Services Law section 366 (5)(d)(1)(i) for transfers between 08/11/1993 and 02/07/2006. See N.Y. Social Services Law section 366 (5)(e)(1)(i) for transfers on or after 02/08/2006. See also 18 NYCRR 360-4.4 (c)(2)(i)(a); Medicaid Reference Guide, at glossary i-ii; 42 U.S.C. section 1396p (h)(1).

To be eligible for Medicaid, the applicant must pursue any potential income and resources that may be available. 18 NYCRR 360-2.3 (c)(1).

Renouncing an inheritance or refusing to assert a right of election are actions which would cause income or resources not to be received. 96 ADM-8, at 6; HCFA Transmittal 64, section 3257 (B).

Since income is an asset, there can be a penalty period for transferring income. 96 ADM-8, at 17; HCFA Transmittal 64, section 3258.6.

"Fair market value" means the estimate of the value of an asset at the prevailing price at the time it was transferred. Medicaid Reference Guide, at glossary vii.

Fair market value of real estate may be established by an appraisal by a real estate broker or other qualified dealer or appraiser. Medicaid Reference Guide, at glossary vii.

"Transfer of assets" means a voluntary assignment of property for less than fair market value. Medicaid Reference Guide, at glossary xxiii.

CALCULATION OF THE PENALTY PERIOD FOR TRANSFERS:

To calculate the penalty period, take (value of transferred asset) ÷ (monthly regional rate) = number of months that Medicaid will not pay the nursing home bill.
96 ADM-8, at 15; Medicaid Reference Guide, at 448. See N.Y. Social Services Law section 366 (5)(d)(4) for transfers made between 08/11/1993 and 2/07/2006. See N.Y. Social Services Law section 366 (5)(e)(5) for transfers made on or after 02/08/2006. See also 18 NYCRR 360-4.4 (c)(2)(iv)(a); 42 U.S.C. section 1396p (c)(1)(E)(1).

Each year, a GIS is issued which tells what the monthly rate is for each region. The state is divided into seven regions. See GIS 11 MA/001 for the 2011 regional rates.

The GIS for 2011 tells which counties are in which region. In prior years, the GIS gave the monthly rate for each region, but did not state which counties were in which region. The attachment to 06 OMM/ADM-2 lists the counties in each region.

During the penalty period, when Medicaid refuses to pay the nursing home bill, the person in the nursing home must pay the actual rate charged by the nursing home. The actual rate charged by the nursing home may be higher than the monthly regional rate which was used to calculate the penalty period.

WHEN THE PENALTY PERIOD BEGINS: THE CURRENT RULE:

The current rule is for transfers made on or after 02/08/2006.

Note that 18 NYCRR 360-4.4 addresses the issue of when the penalty period begins, but it has not been updated since 1996. It does not include the rule for transfers made on or after 02/08/2006. It has the rule for transfers made prior to 02/08/2006.

ONE TRANSFER: The penalty period starts on the first day of the month after which assets were transferred for less than fair market value, OR the first day of the month the otherwise eligible institutionalized individual is receiving nursing facility services for which Medicaid would be available but for the transfer penalty, whichever is later. N.Y. Social Services Law section 366 (5)(e)(5); 06 OMM/ADM 5, at 15-16; GIS 06 MA/016, at 1; 42 U.S.C. section 1396p (c)(1)(D)(ii); Medicaid Reference Guide, at 448.

Example for one transfer:

Person enters the nursing home and a Medicaid application is filed in Broome County on 03/01/2011.

Have you made any transfers since 03/01/2006? Yes.

A transfer of $15,376 was made 12/25/2006.

(Value of transferred asset) ÷ (monthly regional rate) = number of months that Medicaid won't pay.

The 2011 monthly regional rate for Broome County is $7,688 per GIS 11 MA/001.

$15,376 transfer ÷ $7,688 per month = 2 month penalty.

Which 2 months?

We have to compare:

Penalty starts the first day of the month after the assets were transferred: penalty period would be January 2007 and February 2007.

Versus

Penalty starts the first day of the month he is in the nursing home and would be eligible for Medicaid if he had not made the transfer: penalty period would be March 2011 and April 2011.

Which one is later?
March 2011 and April 2011. That is his penalty period.

MULTIPLE TRANSFERS:

Add the transfers together, and divide by the monthly regional rate. 06 OMM/ADM 5, at 5 and 18; GIS 06 MA/016, at 1; Medicaid Reference Guide, at 449. 42 U.S.C. section 1396p (c)(1)(H) allows states to do this. To determine when the penalty period begins, use the same rule that is used when only one transfer was made. See above.

PARTIAL PENALTIES:

see Example # 2 at 06 OMM/ADM 5, at 16. They use $6,872 as a monthly regional rate for the example. Note that this is not a current monthly regional rate.
$30,534 transfer
$30,534 ÷ $6.872 per month = 4.443 month penalty
$6,872 x 4 months = $27,488 penalty for 4 months
$30,354 total transfer - $27,488 penalty for 4 months = $3,046 partial penalty for the 5th month.

See Medicaid Reference Guide at 448-449 for another example of a partial penalty.

A state shall not round down or otherwise disregard any fractional period of ineligibility. 42 U.S.C. section 1396p (c)(1)(E)(iv).

Once a penalty period is established for a transfer, it continues to run even if the person in the nursing home goes home. 96 ADM-8, at 17. If he returns to the nursing home and applies for Medicaid after the penalty period has expired, he will not get another penalty period for that transfer. HCFA Transmittal 64, section 3258.6 (K). Medicaid Reference Guide, at 448.

REDUCING THE VALUE OF THE TRANSFERRED ASSET TO MAKE THE PENALTY PERIOD SHORTER:

Were there outstanding loans, mortgages or other encumbrances on the asset which was transferred? If yes, subtract the loan, mortgage or other encumbrance from the fair market value of the asset when determining the uncompensated value of the transfer. 96 ADM-8, at 11;

Medicaid Reference Guide, at 447 and at glossary xxiv.

Are the applicant's resources below the resource level? If yes, by how much is he below the resource level? Subtract that amount from the fair market value of the asset when determining the uncompensated value of the transfer. 96 ADM-8, at 11; Medicaid Reference Guide, at 447 and glossary xxiv.

Does the applicant have an irrevocable pre-need funeral agreement or burial fund with less than $1500 designated for non-burial space items? If yes, how much less? Subtract that amount from the fair market value of the asset when determining the uncompensated value of the transfer. 96 ADM-8, at 11-12; 90 ADM-36, Attachment A, page 10; Medicaid Reference Guide at 447 and glossary xxiv.

Does the applicant's spouse have a burial fund with less than $1500 designated for non-burial space items? If yes, how much less? Subtract that amount from the fair market value of the asset when determining the uncompensated value of the transfer. 90 ADM-36, Attachment A, page 10.

See also the rules for life estates discussed elsewhere in this book.

The uncompensated value of the transferred asset cannot be reduced by applying it to the CSRA. Medicaid Reference Guide, at 447.

WHEN THE PENALTY PERIOD BEGINS: THE OLD RULE:

The old rule is for transfers made prior to 02/08/2006. You should not be using the old rule unless you are working on a Medicaid application which was filed prior to 02/08/2011.

ONE TRANSFER: the penalty period begins on the first day of the month following the month in which the transfer was made. N.Y. Social Services Law section 366 (5)(d)(4); 18 NYCRR 360-4.4 (c)(2)(iv)(b); 06 OMM/ADM-5, at 15; 96 ADM 8, at 15; 42 U.S.C. section 1396p (c)(1)(D)(i); Medicaid Reference Guide, at 447.

Example for one transfer:

Person enters the nursing home and Medicaid application is filed on 01/03/2011.

Have you made any transfers since 01/03/2006?

Yes. A transfer of $15,376 was made on 02/04/2006.

(Value of transferred asset) ÷ (monthly regional rate) = number of months that Medicaid won't pay.

$15,376 transfer ÷ $7,688 per month = 2 month penalty.

Which 2 months?

The penalty period starts on the first day of the month after the transfer was made.

The transfer was made in February 2006, so the penalty period months are March 2006 and April 2006.

The person was not in the nursing home during March 2006 and April 2006. He has gone past his penalty period. (Under the old rule, it was possible that a penalty period existed on paper but did not hurt you. That possibility has been eliminated under the current rule.)

MULTIPLE TRANSFERS, AND THE PENALTY PERIODS WOULD NOT OVERLAP:

Treat each transfer as a separate event with its own penalty period. The penalty period for each transfer begins on the first day of the month following the month in which the transfer was made. 96 ADM 8, at 16.

MULTIPLE TRANSFERS, AND THE PENALTY PERIODS WOULD OVERLAP:

Add the transfers together, and divide by the monthly regional rate. The penalty period starts the first day of the month following the month in which the first transfer occurred. 96 ADM-8, at 15. 06 OMM/ADM 5, page 15, tells you to see 96 ADM 8. Medicaid Reference Guide, at 449.

PARTIAL PENALTIES:

The uncompensated value becomes part of the Net Available Monthly Income which is owed to the nursing home for one month. 96 ADM-8, at 16.

EXEMPT TRANSFERS

Some transfers are exempt. They do not result in a Medicaid penalty period.

HOMESTEAD TRANSFERRED TO SPOUSE:

There is no penalty period for transferring the homestead to the spouse. See N.Y. Social Services Law section 366 (5)(d)(3)(i)(A) for transfers between 08/11/1993 and 02/07/2006. See N.Y. Social Services Law section 366 (5)(e)(4)(i)(A) for transfers on or after 02/08/2006. See also 18 NYCRR 360-4.4 (c)(2)(iii)(b)(1); 96 ADM-8, at 22; 42 U.S.C. section 1396p (c)(2)(A)(i); HCFA Transmittal 64, section 3258.10(A); Medicaid Reference Guide, at 441.

HOMESTEAD TRANSFERRED TO A CHILD OF THE INDIVIDUAL WHO IS BLIND, DISABLED OR UNDER 21:

There is no penalty period for transferring the homestead to a child of the applicant who is blind, disabled or under age 21. See N.Y. Social Services Law section 366 (5)(d)(3)(i)(B) for transfers between 08/11/1993 and 02/07/2006. See N.Y. Social Services Law section 366 (5)(e)(4)(i)(B) for transfers on or after 02/08/2006. See also 18 NYCRR 360-4.4(c)(2)(iii)(b)(2); 96 ADM-8, at 22; 42 U.S.C. section 1396p (c)(2)(A)(ii); HCFA Transmittal 64, section 3258.10(A); Medicaid Reference Guide, at 442.

DEFINITION OF "BLIND"

When making a transfer to a blind child, the term "blind" has the same meaning given to the term in Social Security Act section 1614 (a)(2). See N.Y. Social Services Law section 366 (5)(d)(1)(ii) for transfers between 08/11/1993 and 02/07/2006. See N.Y. Social Services Law section 366 (5)(e)(1)(1i) for transfers on or after 02/08/2006.

Social Security Act section 1614 (a)(2) is 42 U.S.C. section 1382c (a)(2), which states that a person is considered blind if he has central visual acuity of 20/200 or less in the better eye with use of a correcting lens. An eye has a central visual acuity of 20/200 or less if it is accompanied by a limitation in the field of vision such that the widest diameter of the visual field subtends to an angle no greater than 20 degrees. A person also is considered blind if he is blind under a state plan approved under Title X or XVI (42 U.S.C. section 1201 or 42 section U.S.C. 1301 et seq.) and received aid under such a plan on the basis of blindness for December 1973, so long as he is continuously blind as so defined.

DEFINITION OF "DISABLED"

When making an exempt transfer to a disabled child, the term "disabled" has the same meaning given to the term in Social Security Act section 1614 (a)(3). Medicaid Reference Guide, at glossary v. See N.Y. Social Services Law section 366 (5)(d)(1)(iii) for transfers made between 08/11/1993 and 02/07/2006. See N.Y. Social Services Law section 366 (5)(e)(1)(iii) for transfers made on or after 02/08/2006.

Social Security Act section 1614 (a)(3) is 42 U.S.C. section 1382c (a)(3). 42 U.S.C. section 1382c (a)(3)(A) states that except as provided for in (C), a person is considered to be disabled if he is unable to engage in any substantial gainful activity by reason of any medically determinable physical or mental impairment which can be expected to result in death or which has lasted or can be expected to last for a continuous period of not less than 12 months. 18 NYCRR 360-5.2(b) has the same definition.

42 U.S.C. section 1382c(a)(3)(B) states that an individual shall be determined to be under a disability only if his physical or mental impairment(s) are of such severity that he is not only unable to do his previous work, but cannot, considering his age, education and work experience, engage in any other kind of substantial gainful work which exists in the national economy, regardless of whether such work exists in his immediate area, or whether there is a specific job vacancy, or whether he would be hired if he applied. "Work which exists in the national economy" means that it exists in significant numbers either in the region where the person lives or in several regions of the country.

42 U.S.C. section 1382c (a)(3)(C) states that if the person is under 18,

he shall be considered disabled if he has a medically determinable physical or mental impairment which results in marked and severe functional limitations, and which can be expected to result in death or which has lasted or can be expected to last for a continuous period of not less than 12 months. If a person under 18 engages in substantial gainful activity, he will not be considered disabled.

42 U.S.C. section 1382c (a)(3)(D) states that a physical or mental impairment is one which results from anatomical, physiological or psychological abnormalities which are demonstrated by medically acceptable clinical and laboratory diagnostic techniques.

42 U.S.C. section 1382c (a)(3)(F) states that a person also shall be considered disabled if he is permanently and totally disabled as defined under a state plan approved under Title XIV or Title XVI (42 U.S.C. section 1351 et seq. and 42 U.S.C. section 1381 et seq.), as long as he is continuously disabled as so defined.

42 U.S.C. section 1382(a)(3)(H)(i) states that the provisions of 42 U.S.C. section 221(h), 42 U.S.C. section 221(k) and 42 U.S.C. section 223(d)(5) apply the same as they do when making determinations of disability under Title II (42 U.S.C. section 401 et seq.).

If a Medicaid applicant/recipient transfers an asset to an adult child, and claims that there should not be a penalty period because the adult child is disabled, a Medicaid disability review is to be performed on the adult child. GIS 06 MA/005, at 1; GIS 08 MA/036.

The disability review is to be performed whether the adult child is over 65 or under 65. GIS 08 MA/036. If the adult child is over 65, a disability review packet gets compiled and sent to the State Disability Review Team for determination. If the adult child is under 65, the local Disability Review Team can make the determination. GIS 08 MA/036.

If the adult child has an acceptable disability certification that is currently effective or that was effective at the time of the adult child's 65th birthday, a disability review is not required. GIS 08 MA/036.

GIS 08 MA/036 states that a list of acceptable disability certifications is found in GIS 08 MA/004.

Pages 2 and 3 of GIS 08 MA/004 list the following as acceptable proofs of disability:
- a current disability certification by the State or local Disability Review Team
- a verification of receipt of Railroad Retirement benefits due to total and permanent disability
- a current disability certification by the Social Security Administration for SSDI benefits, including a current award letter, an SSDI benefits check, a bank statement listing an SSDI benefit, or a Medicare card
- a current certification from the Commission for the Blind and Visually Handicapped
- a current letter from the Social Security Administration placing the person in an SSDI Extended Period of Eligibility
- a current letter from the Social Security Administration informing the person that he is no longer eligible for the 1619(b) program.

HOMESTEAD TRANSFERRED TO A SIBLING OF THE INDIVIDUAL WITH AN EQUITY INTEREST:

There is no penalty period for transferring the homestead to a sibling of the applicant if the sibling has an equity interest in the homestead and was residing in the homestead for at least one year immediately before the date that the applicant went into the nursing home. See N.Y. Social Services Law section 366 (5)(d)(3)(i)(C) for transfers between 08/11/1993 and 02/07/2006. See N.Y. Social Services Law section 366 (5)(e)(4)(i)(C) for transfers on or after 02/08/2006. See also 18 NYCRR 360-4.4(c)(2)(iii)(b)(3); 96 ADM-8, at 22; 42 U.S.C. section 1396p (c)(2)(A)(iii); HCFA Transmittal 64, section 3258.10(A); Medicaid Reference Guide, at 442.

HOMESTEAD TRANSFERRED TO A CARETAKER CHILD:

There is no penalty period for transferring the homestead to a child of the applicant if the child was residing in the homestead for at least two years immediately before the date that the applicant went into the nursing home, and the child provided care which let the applicant reside at home rather than having to go into a nursing home. See N.Y. Social Services Law section 366 (5)(d)(3)(i)(D) for transfers between

08/11/1993 and 02/07/2006. See N.Y. Social Services Law section 366 (5)(e)(4)(i)(D) for transfers on or after 02/08/2006. See also 18 NYCRR 360-4.4(c)(2)(iii)(b)(4); 96 ADM-8, at 22; 42 U.S.C. section 1396p (c)(2)(A)(iv); HCFA Transmittal 64, section 3258.10(A); Medicaid Reference Guide, at 442.

The child is referred to as a "Caretaker Child."

It is presumed that the child provided care unless there is evidence to the contrary. Medicaid Reference Guide, at 442. 18 NYCRR 360-4.4(c)(2)(iii)(b)(4) states that "care" is defined in section 311.4(a)(1). 18 NYCRR 311.4(a)(1) states that "care" means "makes arrangements or participates actively in making arrangements for care directly or indirectly, in whole or in part."

ASSETS TRANSFERRED TO SPOUSE:

There is no penalty period for transferring assets to the spouse. See N.Y. Social Services Law section 366 (5)(d)(3)(ii)(A) for transfers between 08/11/1993 and 02/07/2006. See N.Y. Social Services Law section 366 (5)(e)(4)(ii)(A) for transfers on or after 02/08/2006. See also 18 NYCRR 360-4.4(c)(2)(iii)(c)(1)(i); 96 ADM-8, at 22; 42 U.S.C. section 1396p (c)(2)(B)(i); HCFA Transmittal 64, section 3258.10(B); Medicaid Reference Guide, at 442.

ASSETS TRANSFERRED TO ANOTHER FOR THE SOLE BENEFIT OF THE SPOUSE:

There is no penalty period for transferring assets to someone for the sole benefit of the spouse. See N.Y. Social Services Law section 366 (5)(d)(3)(ii)(A) for transfers between 08/11/1993 and 02/07/2006. See N.Y. Social Services Law section 366 (5)(e)(4)(ii)(A) for transfers on or after 02/08/2006. See also 18 NYCRR 360-4.4(c)(2)(iii)(c)(1)(i); 96 ADM-8, at 22; 42 U.S.C. section 1396p (c)(2)(B)(i); HCFA Transmittal 64, section 3258.10(B); Medicaid Reference Guide, at 442.

Does this exemption include the transfer of a homestead? Page 22 of 96 ADM-8 and page 442 of the Medicaid Reference Guide state that this exemption is for the transfer of an asset other than the Medicaid applicant's home. N.Y. Social Services Law, 18 NYCRR and 42 U.S.C. section 1396p do not specify that this exemption is just for transfers other than the homestead.

SOLE BENEFIT:

A transfer is for the sole benefit of someone if the transfer is arranged in such a way that no other individual or entity can benefit from the transferred asset in any way, whether at the time of the transfer or at any time in the future. HCFA Transmittal 64, section 3257 (B)(6).

The transfer must have been accomplished through a written instrument which legally binds the parties to a set course of action and which sets out the conditions under which the transfer was made, and who can benefit from it. HCFA Transmittal 64, section 3258.10 (B)(1).

The instrument or document must provide for spending the funds on a basis that is actuarially sound, based on the life expectancy of the person involved. HCFA Transmittal 64, section 3258.10 (B)(1). The Department of Social Services must conclude that the assets are likely to be totally expended during the spouse's lifetime, based on the spouse's age, the amount transferred, and the rate and amount distributions are made for the spouse 96 ADM-8, at 7-8.

18 NYCRR 360-4.4 (c)(2)(v) defines sole benefit: if terms and conditions of the transfer are specified in a written instrument of transfer executed at or about the time of the transfer, the terms and conditions must clearly limit the use and enjoyment of the property to the spouse. See also 96 ADM-8, at 7.

If there is no written instrument, the person who made the transfer must sign a statement that the transfer was intended for the sole benefit of the spouse, and other evidence must be presented which shows that use and enjoyment in the past has been limited to the spouse. 96 ADM-8, at 7.

Other evidence can include the demonstration of a continuous course of conduct by the person to whom the property was transferred, which shows that the enjoyment of the property has been and will continue to be limited to the spouse. 18 NYCRR 360-4.4 (c)(2)(v). See also 96 ADM-8, at 7.

If the spouse or the person to whom the assets were transferred takes any action which reduces the spouse's beneficial interest in the property, it will be treated as a transfer of assets by the spouse on the date the action was taken. 96 ADM-8, at 8.

If the spouse or the person to whom the assets were transferred takes any action which reduces ownership or control of the person to whom the assets were transferred, it will be treated as a transfer of assets by the spouse on the date the action was taken. 96 ADM-8, at 8.

TRUST FOR SOLE BENEFIT:

A trust is not for the sole benefit of the spouse if the Trustee can make distributions to anyone other than the spouse. 18 NYCRR 360-4.4 (c)(2)(v); 96 ADM-8, at 8.

A trust is not for the sole benefit of the spouse if at the spouse's death principal and income goes to someone other than the Medicaid applicant/recipient's estate or the spouse's estate. 18 NYCRR 360-4.4 (c)(2)(v); 96 ADM-8, at 8.

Medicaid Reference Guide, at 442, states that if there is a remainderman, an asset is not for the "sole benefit" of the spouse.

Page 8 of 96 ADM-8 states that a trust is not for the sole benefit of the spouse if during the life of the trust, the Trustee has the authority to make distributions for the benefit of anyone other than the spouse, or the trust provides that upon termination all or part of the remaining principal and income is to be distributed to someone other than the Medicaid applicant/recipient or the spouse's estate.

A trust is for the sole benefit of someone if the trust benefits no one else, at the time the trust is established and at any time in the future. HCFA Transmittal 64, section 3257 (B)(6).

ASSETS TRANSFERRED FROM THE INDIVIDUAL'S SPOUSE TO ANOTHER FOR THE SOLE BENEFIT OF THE INDIVIDUAL'S SPOUSE:

There is no penalty period for transferring assets from the applicant's spouse to someone else for the sole benefit of the applicant's spouse. See N.Y. Social Services Law section 366 (5)(d)(3)(ii)(B) for transfers between 08/11/1993 and 02/07/2006. See N.Y. Social Services Law section 366 (5)(e)(4)(ii)(B) for transfers on or after 02/08/2006. See also 18 NYCRR 360-4.4(c)(2)(iii)(c)(1)(ii); 96 ADM-8, at 22; Medicaid Reference Guide, at 442; 42 U.S.C. section 1396p (c)(2)(B)(ii); HCFA Transmittal 64, section 3258.10(B).

Does this exemption include the transfer of a homestead? Page 22 of 96 ADM-8 and page 442 of the Medicaid Reference Guide state that this exemption is for the transfer of an asset other than the Medicaid applicant's home. N.Y. Social Services Law, 18 NYCRR and 42 U.S.C. section 1396p do not specify that this exemption is just for transfers other than the homestead.

See above for the "sole benefit" rules.

ASSETS TRANSFERRED TO THE INDIVIDUAL'S CHILD WHO IS BLIND OR DISABLED:

There is no penalty period for transferring assets to the applicant's child who is blind or disabled. See N.Y. Social Services Law section 366 (5)(d)(3)(ii)(C) for transfers between 08/11/1993 and 02/07/2006. See N.Y. Social Services Law section 366 (5)(e)(4)(ii)(C) for transfers on or after 02/08/2006. See also 18 NYCRR 360-4.4(c)(2)(iii)(c)(1)(iii); 96 ADM-8, at 22; 42 U.S.C. section 1396p (c)(2)(B)(iii); HCFA Transmittal 64, section 3258.10(B); Medicaid Reference Guide, at 442.

Does this exemption include the transfer of the homestead to the applicant's child who is blind or disabled? Page 22 of 96 ADM-8 and page 442 of the Medicaid Reference Guide state that this exemption is for the transfer of an asset other than the Medicaid applicant's home. N.Y. Social Services Law, 18 NYCRR and 42 U.S.C. section 1396p do not specify that this exemption is just for transfers other than the homestead.

ASSETS TRANSFERRED TO A TRUST ESTABLISHED SOLELY FOR THE BENEFIT OF THE INDIVIDUAL'S CHILD WHO IS BLIND OR DISABLED:

There is no penalty period for transferring assets to a trust established solely for the benefit of the applicant's child who is blind or disabled. See N.Y. Social Services Law section 366 (5)(d)(3)(ii)(C) for transfers between 08/11/1993 and 02/07/2006. See N.Y. Social Services Law section 366 (5)(e)(4)(ii)(C) for transfers on or after 02/08/2006. See also 18 NYCRR 360-4.4(c)(2)(iii)(c)(1)(iii); 42 U.S.C. section 1396p (c)(2)(B)(iii); HCFA Transmittal 64, section 3258.10 (B).

This exception is not in the Medicaid Reference Guide or 96 ADM-8.

See above for "sole benefit" rules.

ASSETS TRANSFERRED TO A TRUST ESTABLISHED SOLELY FOR THE BENEFIT OF AN INDIVIDUAL UNDER AGE 65 WHO IS DISABLED:

There is no penalty period for transferring assets to a trust established solely for the benefit of a person under age 65 who is disabled. See N.Y. Social Services Law section 366 (5)(d)(3)(ii)(D) for transfers between 08/11/1993 and 02/07/2006. See N.Y. Social Services Law section 366 (5)(e)(4)(ii)(D) for transfers on or after 02/08/2006. See also 18 NYCRR 360-4.4(c)(2)(iii)(c)(1)(iv); 96 ADM-8, at 22; Medicaid Reference Guide, at 442; 42 U.S.C. section 1396p (c)(2)(B)(iv); HCFA Transmittal 64, section 3258.10 (B).

Does this exemption include the transfer of a homestead? Page 22 of 96 ADM-8 and page 442 of the Medicaid Reference Guide state that this exemption is for the transfer of an asset other than the Medicaid applicant's home. N.Y. Social Services Law, 18 NYCRR and 42 U.S.C. section 1396p do not specify that this exemption is just for transfers other than the homestead.

See above for the "sole benefit" rules.

ASSETS TRANSFERRED TO PURCHASE A LIFE ESTATE IN SOMEONE ELSE'S HOME AFTER 02/08/2006:

There is no penalty period for transferring assets to purchase a life estate in someone else's home after 02/08/2006, if the applicant lives in the home for at least one year after purchasing the life estate in that home.

How long is a year? The Deficit Reduction Act states, "for a period of at least 1 year." 42 U.S.C. section 1396p(c)(1)(J). The New York statute states, "for a period of at least 1 year." N.Y. Social Services Law section 366 (5)(e)(3)(ii). Pages 23-24 of 06 OMM/ADM-5 state, "for at least a continuous period of one year." Page 2 of GIS 06 MA/016, at 2 states, "for a period of at least one year." Pages 354 and 443 of the Medicaid Reference Guide state, "for at least a continuous period of one year."

The "continuous" language could be problematic if the applicant spent part of the year somewhere else, such as someone who stayed in Florida for several months during the winter.

APPLICANT OR SPOUSE INTENDED TO GET FAIR MARKET VALUE:

There is no penalty period for transferring assets if a satisfactory showing is made that the applicant or the spouse intended to dispose of the assets either at fair market value, or for other valuable consideration. For transfers between 08/11/1993 and 02/07/2006, see N.Y. Social Services Law section 366 (5)(d)(3)(iii)(A). For transfers on or after 02/08/2006, see N.Y. Social Services Law section 366 (5)(e)(4)(iii)(A). See also 18 NYCRR 360-4.4(c)(2)(iii)(d)(i); 96 ADM-8, at 22; 42 U.S.C. section 1396p (c)(2)(C)(i); Medicaid Reference Guide, at 443.

HCFA Transmittal 64, at 3258.10 (C)(1) advises that the applicant should have to provide written evidence of attempts to dispose of the asset at fair market value, and evidence to support the value, if any, at which the asset was sold.

ASSETS WERE TRANSFERRED EXCLUSIVELY FOR A PURPOSE OTHER THAN TO QUALIFY FOR MEDICAID:

There is no penalty period if a satisfactory showing is made that the assets were transferred exclusively for a purpose other than to qualify for Medicaid. For transfers between 08/11/1993 and 02/07/2006, see N.Y. Social Services Law section 366 (5)(d)(3)(iii)(B). For transfers on or after 02/08/2006, see N.Y. Social Services Law section 366 (5)(e)(4)(iii)(B). See also 18 NYCRR 360-4.4(c)(2)(iii)(d)(ii); 96 ADM-8, page 23; 42 U.S.C. section 1396p (c)(2)(C)(ii); HCFA Transmittal 64, section 3258.10 (C); Fair hearings include In re Appeal of J.V., Fair Hearing # 4898029L (03/14/2008) and In re Appeal of M.L. (07/18/2008).

The Department of Social Services must not take any adverse action on an applicant/recipient who transferred assets without first advising him in writing of his right to show that the transfer was made exclusively for a purpose other than to qualify for Medicaid. 96 ADM-8, at 23.

The applicant or the spouse is allowed a minimum of 20 days to present evidence that a transfer was made exclusively for a purpose other than to qualify for Medicaid. Medicaid Reference Guide, at 445.

Page 445 of the Medicaid Reference Guide states that some factors suggesting that a transfer was made exclusively for a purpose other than to qualify for Medicaid include: the traumatic onset of a disability after the transfer, such as a heart attack with no previous record of heart disease; the unexpected loss of other resources which would have precluded Medicaid eligibility.

Page 23 of 96 ADM-8 states that factors suggesting that a transfer was made exclusively for a purpose other than to qualify for Medicaid include: the unexpected onset of a serious medical condition after the transfer; the unexpected loss, after the transfer, of income or resources which would have been sufficient to pay for nursing home care; the existence of a court order requiring the transfer of assets.

If assets are transferred, there is a rebuttable presumption that they were transferred for the purpose of establishing or maintaining Medicaid eligibility. The presumption is rebutted only if the individual provides convincing evidence that the resources were transferred exclusively for a purpose other than to qualify or remain eligible for Medicaid. Medicaid Reference Guide, at 445.

If the person had some other purpose for making the transfer but an expectation of establishing and maintaining Medicaid eligibility also was a factor, the transfer will result in a penalty period. Medicaid Reference Guide, at 445.

The applicant must provide convincing evidence that the transfer was made exclusively for a purpose other than to qualify for Medicaid. The person's signed statement regarding the circumstances of the transfer should include: purpose for making the transfer; attempts, if any, to dispose of the asset at fair market value; the reason for accepting less than fair market value; means or plan for supporting himself after the transfer; relationship to the person who received the transferred asset; belief that the person did receive fair market value for the asset (if applicable). Medicaid Reference Guide, at 445-46.

A signed statement from the person is not, by itself, convincing evidence. Pertinent documentary evidence includes, but is not limited to, legal documents, real estate agreements, correspondence and medical reports. Medicaid Reference Guide, at 446.

All of the circumstances of the transfer will be considered, as well as the person's age, health and financial situation at the time the transfer was made. 96 ADM-8, Attachment III, page 4.

A transfer is presumed to have been made for the purpose of qualifying for Medicaid if it was made one year or less before the Medicaid application was filed. N.Y. Social Services Law section 104-a.

ASSETS WERE RETURNED:

There is no penalty period if all assets transferred for less than fair market value were returned. For transfers between 08/11/1993 and

02/07/2006, see N.Y. Social Services Law section 366 (5)(d)(3)(iii)(C). For transfers on or after 02/08/2006, see N.Y. Social Services Law section 366 (5)(e)(4)(iii)(C). See also 18 NYCRR 360-.4(c)(2)(iii)(d)(iii); 06 OMM/ADM-5, at 18-19; 96 ADM-8, at 23; 42 U.S.C. section 1396p (c)(2)(C)(iii); HCFA Transmittal 64, section 3258.10 (C); Medicaid Reference Guide, at 443.

Note that although the rule seems to specify the return of all assets, page 443 of the Medicaid Reference Guide and HCFA Transmittal 64, section 3258.10 (C)(3) state that if a portion of the transferred assets is returned after Medicaid eligibility is determined, the penalty period will be recalculated.

UNDUE HARDSHIP:

For transfers made between 08/11/1993 and 02/07/2006, there is no penalty period if denial of Medicaid eligibility would cause an undue hardship. N.Y. Social Services Law section 366 (5)(d)(3)(iv); 18 NYCRR 360-4.4 (c)(2)(iii)(3).

Undue hardship occurs when the person: is otherwise eligible for Medicaid; is unable to obtain appropriate medical care without Medicaid; is unable to have the transferred assets returned, or to receive fair market value for them, despite the best efforts of the person and/or the spouse. "Best efforts" includes cooperating in the pursuit of the return of the assets. 06 OMM/ADM 5, at 19-20; 18 NYCRR 360-4.4(c)(2)(iii)(e); Medicaid Reference Guide, at 446.

For transfers made on or after 02/08/2006, there is no penalty period if denial of Medicaid eligibility would deprive the applicant of medical care such that his health or life would be endangered, *or* would deprive him of food, clothing, shelter, or other necessities of life. N.Y. Social Services Law section 366 (5)(e)(4)(iv); 06 OMM/ADM-5, at 19-20. Page 448 of Medicaid Reference Guide uses the word "and" rather than "or."

See also 42 U.S.C. section 1396p(c)(2)(D).

Undue hardship cannot be claimed if the applicant failed to fully cooperate to the best of his ability in having all of the transferred assets returned, or the trust declared void. Cooperation includes, but is not limited to, assisting in providing all legal records pertaining to the transfer or trust creation, providing information regarding the amount transferred, providing documents to support the transfer, and providing information regarding the circumstances of the transfer. 06 OMM/ADM-5, at 20; 90 ADM-8, at 23.

Undue hardship cannot be claimed merely because the individual or spouse would be unable to maintain a pre-existing lifestyle. 06 OMM/ADM-5, at 20; 96 ADM-8, at 23.

Page 4 of 90 ADM-29 states that previously, undue hardship did not exist if the resource was transferred to any relative of the individual. That distinction was eliminated due to the possibility that a person might have been coerced into making a transfer due to actual or threatened abuse. Also, the transfer might not have been authorized by the applicant, or might have been made without his knowledge.

ASSETS TRANSFERRED TO PURCHASE LOANS, PROMISSORY NOTES & MORTGAGES:

N.Y. Social Services Law section 366 (5)(e)(3)(iii) states that the purchase of a promissory note, loan or mortgage shall be treated as the disposal of an asset for less than fair market value unless the note, loan, or mortgage meets the requirements of section 1917 (c)(1)(I) of the Federal Social Security act. Note that N.Y. Social Services Law section 366 (5)(e) is for transfers made on or after 02/08/06.

Section 1917(c)(1)(I) of the Federal Social Security Act is 42 U.S.C. 1396p (c)(1)(I). It provides that there is no penalty period if the loan/note/mortgage: has a repayment term that is actuarially sound as determined in accordance with actuarial publications of the Office of the Chief Actuary of the Social Security Administration; provides for payments to be made in equal amounts during the term of the loan, with no deferral and no balloon payments made; and prohibits the cancellation of the balance upon the death of the lender. See also 06 OMM/ADM-5, at 7 and 24; Medicaid Reference Guide, at 443.

If a promissory note, loan or mortgage does not satisfy those requirements, the amount of the transfer is the outstanding balance due at the time the Medicaid application is filed. Medicaid Reference Guide, at 443; 42 U.S.C. section 1396p (c)(1)(I).

ASSETS TRANSFERRED ACCORDING TO TERMS OF PERSONAL SERVICE CONTRACTS:

While relatives and family members can be paid when they provide care, there is a presumption that services provided for free at the time were intended to be provided without compensation. Thus, a transfer to a relative for care provided for free in the past normally is a transfer of assets for less than fair market value, and will result in a penalty period. However, an individual can rebut this presumption with tangible evidence. 96 ADM-8, at 12; HCFA Transmittal 64, section 3258.1(A)(1).

A personal services contract, also known as a caregiver agreement, is a formal written agreement between two or more parties. One of the parties agrees to provide personal and/or managerial services in exchange for compensation. GIS 07 MA/019, at 1.

If a Medicaid applicant has a personal services contract, the Department of Social Services must determine whether the applicant received or will receive fair market value for the assets transferred to the caregiver. GIS 07 MA/109, at 1.

If a determination cannot be made that the applicant will receive fair market value in exchange for the assets transferred to the caregiver, the assets which were transferred are subject to a transfer penalty. GIS 07 MA/019, at 1.

If the personal services contract does not provide for the return of any prepaid money if the caretaker cannot fulfill his duties under the contract or if the Medicaid applicant dies before his life expectancy: this will be treated as a transfer of assets for less than fair market value and will be subject to a penalty period. GIS 07 MA/019, at 1; Medicaid Reference Guide, at 444.

If the contract provides for the return of funds if the caretaker cannot fulfill his duties under the contract or if the applicant dies before his life expectancy: the Department of Social Services still needs to determine if the applicant will receive fair market value in exchange for the funds transferred to the caregiver. Medicaid Reference Guide, at 444.

If the personal services contract provides that services will be delivered on an "as needed" basis, there will be a penalty period. GIS 07 MA/019, at 1; Medicaid Reference Guide, at 444.

When calculating the penalty period, the transfer amount gets reduced by the value of services which were provided between the date the contract was signed and funded through the date the person became eligible for Medicaid. GIS 07 MA/019, at 2; Medicaid Reference Guide, at 444. But if the services in the contract are part of the Medicaid nursing home rate, no credit is allowed. GIS 07 MA/019, at 2; Medicaid Reference Guide, at 444.

The Department of Social Services must be given documentation, such as a log with dates and times that the caregiver provided services. GIS 07 MA/019, at 2; Medicaid Reference Guide, at 444.

The value of the caregiver's services must be commensurate with a reasonable wage scale, based on fair market value for the actual job performed and the caregiver's qualifications. The U.S. Department of Labor, Bureau of Labor Statistics, Occupational Outlook Handbook may be used by the Department of Social Services to value the caregiver's services. GIS 07 MA/019, at 2; Medicaid Reference Guide, at 444. The handbook may be found at www.bls.gov/oco/.

TRUSTS

If the Medicaid applicant or spouse created a trust or is the beneficiary of a trust, two questions arise:

Does the trust count when determining Medicaid financial eligibility?

Does funding the trust create a Medicaid penalty period?

The answers to these questions are based on the type of trust that was created, and who created it.

THE LOOK-BACK PERIOD FOR TRUSTS:

The look-back period for trusts is sixty months. 96 ADM-8, at 12; N.Y. Social Services Law sections 366 (5)(d)(i)(vi) and 366 (5)(e)(i)(vi); 06 OMM/ADM-5, at 5.

The Access NY Supplement A part of the Medicaid application asks, "In the last 60 months, have you or your spouse created or transferred any assets into or out of a trust?"

Funding a new trust is a trust-related transfer. 96 ADM-8, at 2.

Transferring assets into an existing trust is a trust-related transfer. 96 ADM-8, at 12.

Making distributions from a trust to someone other than the Medicaid applicant is a trust-related transfer. 96 ADM-8, at 12.

However, not all trust-related transfers result in a penalty period.

PENALTY PERIODS FOR TRUSTS:

If there is a penalty period, it is calculated the same way penalty periods are calculated when a transfer is made for less than fair market value: (value of transferred asset) ÷ (monthly regional rate) = number of months that Medicaid will not pay the nursing home bill.

See GIS 11 MA/001 for the 2011 regional rates. Calculation of penalty periods is discussed elsewhere in this book.

If there is a penalty period, the starting time is determined the same way it would be determined when a transfer is made for less than fair market value. That is discussed elsewhere in this book.

IRREVOCABLE INTER VIVOS TRUSTS:

An irrevocable inter vivos trust is a trust that cannot be cancelled by the person who created it. 96 ADM-8, at 10; 92 ADM-45, at 3; Medicaid Reference Guide, at 361. The trust begins and is effective while the creator is alive.

If the applicant or the spouse created an irrevocable inter vivos trust, and if payments of principal cannot be made from the trust to the applicant, the trust principal does not count when determining Medicaid financial eligibility. See N.Y. Social Services Law section 366 (5)(d)(6) for transfers to this type of trust made between 08/10/1993 and 02/07/2006. See N.Y. Social Services Law section 366 (5)(e)(7) for transfers to this type of trust made on or after 02/08/2006. See also N.Y. Social Services Law section 366 (2)(b)(2)(ii); 18 NYCRR 360-4.5 (b)(1) and (3); HCFA Transmittal 64, section 3258.4 (E) and 3259.6(B); Medicaid Reference Guide, at 361-62.

However, there is a penalty period for assets put into the trust during the look-back period. See N.Y. Social Services Law section 366 (5)(d)(6) for transfers to this type of trust made between 08/10/1993 and 02/07/2006. See N.Y. Social Services Law section 366 (5)(e)(7) for transfers to this type of trust made on or after 02/08/2006. See also N.Y. Social Services Law section 366 (2)(b)(2)(ii); 18 NYCRR 360-4.5 (b)(1) and (3); HCFA Transmittal 64, section 3258.4 (E) and 3259.6(B); Medicaid Reference Guide, at 361-62.

If payment of principal can be made from the trust to the applicant, the trust principal does count when determining Medicaid financial eligibility. 96 ADM-8, at 13; 42 U.S.C. section 1396p (d)(3)(B).

There is a penalty period for any payment which could have been given to the Medicaid applicant but which was given to someone else. See N.Y. Social Services Law section 366 (5)(d)(6) for payments made between 08/10/1993 and 02/07/2006. See N.Y. Social Services Law section 366 (5)(e)(7) for payments made on or after 02/08/2006. See also N.Y. Social Services Law section 366 (2)(b)(2)(ii); 18 NYCRR 360-4.5 (b)(1) and (3); 96 ADM-8, at 13; 42 U.S.C. section 1396p (d)(3)(B); HCFA Transmittal 64, section 3258.4 (E) and 3259.6(B); Medicaid Reference Guide, at 362.

Distributions from the trust are treated as income. See N.Y. Social Services Law section 366 (5)(d)(6) for distributions made between 08/10/1993 and 02/07/2006. See N.Y. Social Services Law section 366 (5)(e)(7) for distributions made on or after 02/08/2006. See also N.Y. Social Services Law section 366 (2)(b)(2)(ii); 18 NYCRR 360-4.5 (b)(1) and (3); 96 ADM-8, at 13; 42 U.S.C. section 1396p (d)(3)(B); HCFA Transmittal 64, section 3258.4 (E) and 3259.6(B); Medicaid Reference Guide, at 362.

GIS 04 MA/001 advises social service districts that Verdow v. Sutkowy and Spetz v. N.Y. State Dep't of Health prevent them from treating an irrevocable trust as an available resource merely because the creator retained a limited power of appointment. See Verdow v. Sutkowy, 209 F.R.D. 309 (2002) and Spetz v. N.Y. State Dep't of Health, 190 Misc. 2d 297 (2002), appeal dismissed 302 A.D.2d 1019 (2003).

When determining a penalty period, the date of the transfer is the date the trust was established or the date upon which payment to the grantor was foreclosed. HCFA Transmittal 64, section 3258.4 (E).

REVOCABLE INTER VIVOS TRUSTS:

A revocable trust is a trust that can be cancelled by the person who created it. See 96 ADM-8, at 10; Medicaid Reference Guide, at 362. The trust begins and is effective while the creator is alive.

If the applicant or the spouse created a revocable inter vivos trust, the trust principal does count when determining Medicaid financial eligibility

There is no penalty period for putting assets into a revocable trust. There is a penalty period for payments made from the trust to someone other than the Medicaid applicant.

Distributions from the trust are treated as income.

See N.Y. Social Services Law section 366 (5)(d)(6) for transfers to this type of trust made between 08/10/1993 and 02/07/2006. See N.Y. Social Services Law section 366 (5)(e)(7) for transfers to this type of trust made on or after 02/08/2006. See also N.Y. Social Services Law section 366 (2)(b)(2)(i); 18 NYCRR 360-4.5(b)(2) and (3); 42 U.S.C. section 1396p (d)(3)(A); HCFA Transmittal 64, sections 3258.4 (E) and 3259.6(A); Medicaid Reference Guide, at 362.

PAYBACK TRUSTS:

A payback trust is a trust that contains the assets of a disabled person. The trust was created for the benefit of the disabled person when the disabled person was under the age of sixty-five. The trust was created by the disabled person's parent, grandparent, legal guardian, or a court of competent jurisdiction. The Trust Agreement states that when the disabled person dies, the State must receive everything remaining in the trust, up to the total value of Medical Assistance paid by the State on behalf of the disabled person. N.Y. Social Services Law section 366(2)(b)(2)(iii)(A); 18 NCYRR 360-4.5 (b)(5)(i)(a); 96 ADM-8, at 9 and 13; 42 U.S.C. section 1396p (d)(4)(A); Medicaid Reference Guide, at 359.

If all of the above requirements are met, the trust principal does not count when determining Medicaid financial eligibility. N.Y. Social Services Law section 366(2)(b)(2)(iii)(A); 18 NCYRR 360-4.5 (b)(5)(i)(a); 96 ADM-8, at 9 and 13; 42 U.S.C. section 1396p (d)(4)(A); Medicaid Reference Guide, at 359.

Additions to the trust made after the age of sixty-five are subject to a penalty period. 96 ADM-8, at 9; HCFA Transmittal 64, section 3259.7(A); Medicaid Reference Guide, at 359.

If all of the above requirements are met, income held in the trust is not available income. N.Y. Social Services Law section 366(2)(b)(2)(iii)(A); 18 NCYRR 360-4.5 (b)(5)(i)(a); 96 ADM-8, at 9 and 13; 42 U.S.C. section 1396p (d)(4)(A); Medicaid Reference Guide, at 359.

Distributions from the trust are treated as income. 96 ADM-8, at 14; Medicaid Reference Guide, at 359.

18 NYCRR 360-4.5 (b)(5)(iii) has additional requirements for Payback Trusts and Pooled Trusts. The Trustee must notify the Department of Social Services that the trust was created or funded. The Trustee must notify the Department of Social Services when the beneficiary dies. If the trust has a value of $100,000 to $500,000 the Trustee must notify the Department of Social Services of transactions which will deplete the trust by 5%. If the trust has a value of $500,001 to $1,000,000 the Trustee must notify the Department of Social Services of transactions which will deplete the trust by 10%. If the trust has a value of more than $1,000,000 the Trustee must notify the Department of Social Services of transactions which will deplete the trust by 15%. The Trustee must notify the Department of Social Services in advance of transfers of trust principal for less than fair market value. If the trust has assets of $1,000,000 or more the Trustee must give the Department of Social Services proof of bonding, unless a court has waived the bonding requirement. If the trust has assets of less than $1,000,000 and a court required a bond, the Trustee must give the Department of Social Services proof of the bond. See also 96 ADM-8, at 14.

POOLED TRUSTS:

A pooled trust is a trust that contains the assets of a disabled person. The trust is established and managed by a non-profit association. The non-profit maintains separate accounts for the benefit of disabled individuals, but pools the accounts for investment and management purposes. Each account in the trust is established for the benefit of the disabled person by the disabled person himself or by the parent, grandparent, legal guardian or a court of competent jurisdiction. When the disabled person dies, the non-profit can keep any funds left in the disabled person's account. If the non-profit does not keep the funds left in the account, the funds must be paid to the State, up to the total value of all Medical Assistance paid by the State on behalf of the disabled person. Social Services Law section 366 (2)(b)(2)(iii)(B); 18 NCYRR 360-4.5 (b)(5)(i)(b); 96 ADM-8, at 9-10 and 14; GIS 08 MA/020; 42 U.S.C. section 1396p (d)(4)(C).

If all of the above requirements are met, the trust principal does not count when determining Medicaid financial eligibility. Social Services Law section 366 (2)(b)(2)(iii)(B); 18 NCYRR 360-4.5 (b)(5)(i)(b); 96 ADM-8, at 9-10 and 14; GIS 08 MA/020; 42 U.S.C. section 1396p (d)(4)(C).

If all of the above requirements are met, income held in the trust is not available income. Social Services Law section 366 (2)(b)(2)(iii)(B); 18 NCYRR 360-4.5 (b)(5)(i)(b); 96 ADM-8, at 9-10 and 14; GIS 08 MA/020; 42 U.S.C. section 1396p (d)(4)(C).

Distributions from the trust are available income. 96 ADM-8, at 14; Medicaid Reference Guide, at 359.

Additions to the trust made after the age of sixty-five are subject to a penalty period. 96 ADM-8, at 10; GIS 08 MA/020; 06 OMM/INF-1, at 2; HCFA Transmittal 64, section 3259.7 (B); Medicaid Reference Guide, at 360.

Note that penalty periods are for the transfer of an asset for less than fair market value. N.Y. Social Services Law section 366 (5)(d)(3) for transfers made between 08/11/1993 and 02/07/2006; N.Y. Social Services Law section 366 (5)(e)(3) for transfers made on or after 02/08/2006. GIS 08 MA/020 reminds us that an addition to a pooled trust might be a transfer for fair market value, and thus would not be subject to a penalty period.

Example 1 from GIS 08 MA/020:
A 68-year-old disabled person living in the community has a pooled trust. After age 65, he put income of $825 per month for 10 months into the trust. $825 x 10 = $8,250. He then goes into a nursing home. The $8,250 is considered a transfer.
If the trust paid $700 per month for his rent and $125 per month for his household utilities during those 10 months, he received a benefit of $700 + $125 = $825 x 10 = $8,250. His $8,250 transfer was a transfer for fair market value; no penalty period.

Example 2:
A 68-year-old disabled person living in the community has a pooled trust. After age 65, he put income of $825 per month for 10 months into the trust. $825 x 10 = $8,250. He then goes into a nursing home. The $8,250 is considered a transfer.

If the trust paid $600 per month for his rent and $100 per month for his household utilities during those 10 months, he received a benefit of $600 + $100 + $700 x 10 = $7,000. $7,000 of his $8,250 transfer was a transfer for fair market value; no penalty period. But the remaining $1,250 of his transfer was not a transfer for fair market value and is subject to a penalty period.

18 NYCRR 360-4.5 (b)(5)(iii) has additional requirements for Payback Trusts and Pooled Trusts. The Trustee must notify the Department of Social Services that the trust was created or funded. The Trustee must notify the Department of Social Services when the beneficiary dies. If the trust has a value of $100,000 to $500,000 the Trustee must notify the Department of Social Services of transactions which will deplete the trust by 5%. If the trust has a value of $500,001 to $1,000,000 the Trustee must notify the Department of Social Services of transactions which will deplete the trust by 10%. If the trust has a value of more than $1,000,000 the Trustee must notify the Department of Social Services of transactions which will deplete the trust by 15%. The Trustee must notify the Department of Social Services in advance of transfers of trust principal for less than fair market value. If the trust has assets of $1,000,000 or more the Trustee must give the Department of Social Services proof of bonding, unless a court has waived the bonding requirement. If the trust has assets of less than $1,000,000 and a court required a bond, the Trustee must give the Department of Social Services proof of the bond. See also 96 ADM-8, at 14.

THIRD PARTY INTER VIVOS TRUSTS:

A third party trust is a trust that was created with funds belonging to someone other than the Medicaid applicant. The trust principal does not count when determining Medicaid financial eligibility. Distributions from the trust are available income. 96 ADM-8, at 11; 18 NYCRR 360-4.5(b)(4); Medicaid Reference Guide, at 363-64.

TESTAMENTARY TRUSTS:

A testamentary trust is a trust that was created by Will. It does not exist until after the creator dies. The trust principal does not count when determining Medicaid financial eligibility. Distributions from the trust are available income. 18 NYCRR 360-4.5(c); 96 ADM-8, at 11; Medicaid Reference Guide, at 363-64. Income held in the trust is not available income. 96 ADM-8, at 11; Medicaid Reference Guide, at 364.

SUPPLEMENTAL NEEDS TRUSTS:

A supplemental needs trust is a discretionary trusts that was established for the benefit of a person with a severe and chronic or persistent disability. These trusts are intended to supplement, not supplant, government benefits or assistance. EPTL 7-1.12.

If the Supplemental Needs Trust was created under someone's Will: see the rules for Testamentary Trusts.

If the Supplemental Needs Trust was created by someone while alive and was funded with assets of someone other than the disabled person: see the rules for Third Party Inter Vivos Trusts.

If the Supplemental Needs Trust was funded with assets of the disabled person: see the rules for Payback Trusts and Pooled Trusts.

If the Supplemental Needs Trust was funded with assets of the disabled person and is not a Payback Trust or a Pooled Trust: see the rules for Irrevocable Inter Vivos Trusts.

TRIGGER TRUSTS:

A trigger trust begins and is effective when the creator is alive. The trust instrument provides that the grantor's interest in the trust will terminate if he goes into a nursing home. Trigger trusts are inter vivos trusts. N.Y. Estates, Powers and Trusts Law (EPTL) section 7-3.1 (c) provides that this type of trust is void as against public policy. EPTL 7-

3.1 (c) only applies to trusts created on or after 04/02/1992. 92 ADM-45, at 5. Trigger Trusts created prior to that date are not void. See also 18 NYCRR 360-4.5(d); 92 ADM-45, at 2 and 4. When a Trigger Trust is void, the assets in the trust count when determining Medicaid financial eligibility. 96 ADM-8, at 13.

MEDICAID INCOME RULES

If Medicaid is paying someone's nursing home bill, there are rules about how much income the person can keep, and how much income the community spouse can keep. The rest of their income is supposed to go to the nursing home each month. The amount that goes to the nursing home is referred to as the Net Available Monthly Income (NAMI).

The Department of Social Services calculates the NAMI when the Medicaid application is filed. The Department of Social Services re-calculates the NAMI whenever there is a change to the income or health insurance premiums of the applicant or the community spouse.

Income is any payment received by the Medicaid applicant/recipient, from any source. 18 NYCRR 360-4.3(b)(1); Medicaid Reference Guide, at 103.

Income includes payments of money, goods or services. 18 NYCRR 360-4.3(b)(1).

Earned income is income received as a result of work activity. This includes wages, salaries, tips, commissions and income from self-employment. 18 NYCRR 360-4.3(b)(2); Medicaid Reference Guide, at 104.

Unearned income is income that is not received as compensation for work performed. 18 NYCRR 360-4.3(b)(3). Unearned income is paid due to a legal or moral obligation rather than for current services performed. Unearned income includes pensions, government benefits, dividends, interest, insurance compensation and other types of payments. 18 NYCRR 360-4.3(b)(3); Medicaid Reference Guide, at 121. It includes cash contributions from friends and relatives who are not legally responsible relatives. Medicaid Reference Guide, at 142.

In-kind income is income received in goods and services rather than money. 18 NYCRR 360-4.3(b)(4). If in-kind income is not the result of working, and does not come from a legally responsible relative who lives outside the household, it is not treated as available income. 18 NYCRR 360-4.3(e)(1); Medicaid Reference Guide, at 150-51.

Gifts are not income, but they can be resources. 18 NYCRR 360-4.3 (e)(1).

Deductions such as taxes and FICA generally are not disregarded for Medicaid purposes. Medicaid Reference Guide, at 103 and 104. The Medicaid income contribution generally is calculated based on the amount before these deductions are taken.

When both husband and wife are in permanent absent status, they are budgeted as individuals. Medicaid Reference Guide, at 285 and 399.

INCOME -- MONTH ONE -- PERSON IN A NURSING HOME WHO DOES NOT HAVE A COMMUNITY SPOUSE

If the applicant does not have a community spouse, he and any persons residing in his former household are budgeted as a community household for the first month or partial month of permanent absence. Appropriate disregards are used to determine monthly net income. The monthly income of him and his household (if any) is compared to the Medically Needy Income Level or Medicaid Standard (and MBL Living Arrangement Chart, as appropriate), whichever is most beneficial. Medicaid Reference Guide, at 285.

The Medicaid Standard is not used for SSI-related people, who are the subject of this book. It is used to determine eligibility for Single/Childless Couples (who are not yet 65) and Low Income Families (families with children, children under 21 who are not living with a caretaker relative, applying caretaker relatives, including adult cases, and pregnant women).

18 NYCRR 360-4.10(b)(3) states that the net income of the person in the nursing home per 18 NYCRR 360-4.3(a)(1) and (2) shall be compared with the appropriate MA [Medical Assistance] or PA [Public Assistance] income standard for one person. Note that 18 NYCRR 360-4.10 was last updated in 1997. GIS 08 MA/022, dated April 1, 2008, states that after the standardization of the levels for the S/CC and LIF populations, the PA Standard of Need will not be used for eligibility determinations after April 1, 2008.

Thus, the Medically Needy Income Level is the appropriate standard. The Medically Needy Income Level for a household of one for 2011 is $767 per month. GIS 10 MA/026.

Some types of income do not count. See the discussion of Income Disregards for month one for a person in a nursing home.

INCOME -- MONTH ONE -- PERSON IN A NURSING HOME WHO DOES HAVE A COMMUNITY SPOUSE

If the applicant does have a community spouse, determine his income, then subtract SSI-related disregards to arrive at his countable monthly income for the first month in the nursing home. Subtract the Medically Needy Income level for one or the Medicaid Standard for one, whichever is higher. Medicaid Reference Guide, at 280.

The Medicaid Standard is not used for SSI-related people, who are the subject of this book. It is used to determine eligibility for Single/Childless Couples (who are not yet 65) and Low Income Families (families with children, children under 21 who are not living with a caretaker relative, applying caretaker relatives, including adult cases, and pregnant women).

18 NYCRR 360-4.10(b)(3) states that if the person in the nursing home has a community spouse: for the first month or partial month in the nursing home, compare his net available income, and any income actually contributed by the community spouse, to the appropriate MA [Medical Assistance] or PA [Public Assistance] income standard for one person. Note that 18 NYCRR 360-4.10 was last updated in 1997. GIS 08 MA/022, dated April 1, 2008, states that after the standardization of the levels for the S/CC and LIF populations, the PA Standard of Need will not be used for eligibility determinations after April 1, 2008.

Thus, the Medically Needy Income Level is the appropriate standard. The Medically Needy Income Level for a household of one for 2011 is $767 per month. GIS 10 MA/026.

Some types of income do not count. A discussion of income disregards follows.

INCOME DISREGARDS -- MONTH ONE -- PERSON IN A NURSING HOME

Certain types of income are disregarded during the first month that the applicant is in the nursing home.

18 NYCRR 360-4.6 (a) lists income disregards for all Medicaid applicants/recipients.

18 NYCRR 360-4.6 (a)(2) lists additional income disregards for people in the SSI-Related category.

The Medicaid Reference Guide has some SSI-Related Income Disregards which are not included in 18 NYCRR 360-4.6 (a)(2).

AMERICORPS:

Child care allowances and other benefits/services provided by Americorps USA and Americorps NCCC are disregarded, except payments for living expenses. Medicaid Reference Guide, at 220. See also Volunteer Payments for Americorps VISTA payments.

AGENT ORANGE:

Payments from the Agent Orange Settlement Fund or any other fund under the Agent Orange product liability litigation settlement, and payments received from court proceedings brought for personal injuries sustained by veterans resulting from exposure to dioxin or phenoxy herbicides in connection with the war in Indochina from January 1, 1962 through May 7, 1975, are disregarded. 18 NYCRR 360-4.6(a)(1)(xxii); 91 ADM-8; Medicaid Reference Guide, at 229.

BLOOD PLASMA SETTLEMENTS:

Payments received as a result of a federal class action settlement with four manufacturers of blood plasma products on behalf of hemophilia patients who are infected with HIV are disregarded. Medicaid

Reference Guide, at 220.

BOARDER INCOME:

The first $90 per month of income received from a person living in the home who is not a family member is disregarded. If the family can document out-of-pocket expenses greater than $90 per month incurred in providing room and board, the value of these documented expenses also will be disregarded. 18 NYCRR 360-4.6(a)(1)(xvii); Medicaid Reference Guide, at 118-19 and 227.

BURIAL FUND INTEREST:

Interest earned on excluded burial funds and appreciation in the value of an excluded burial arrangement which are to become part of the separately identifiable burial fund are disregarded. 18 NYCRR 360-4.6(a)(2)(xvii); Medicaid Reference Guide, at 221.

BUSINESS EXPENSES:

Business expenses which can be deducted from self-employment income or from income from a small business which the person owns and operates are:
(1) rent
(2) employee salaries and fringe benefits
(3) cost of goods for resale
(4) business taxes
(5) licenses and permits
(6) cost of tools, supplies and raw materials
(7) insurance for the business
(8) lights, heat, water, sewage and phone charges
(9) advertising
(10) travel
(11) taxes and carrying charges on property used in the business, other than payments of mortgage principal
(12) depreciation costs for buildings, equipment and materials necessary for and directly related to operation of the business

(13) any other expenses necessary for and directly related to operation of the business. 18 NYCRR 360-4.3(c).

CENSUS EMPLOYMENT EARNINGS:

Earnings from census employment are disregarded. Medicaid Reference Guide, at 228.

CERTIFIED BLIND REASONABLE WORK-RELATED EXPENSES:

All remaining reasonable work-related expenses for certified blind people, including mandatory retirement deductions after other disregards, are disregarded. Medicaid Reference Guide, at 221.

CHILD CARE:

Payments made for child care services, or the value of any child care services provided to a recipient of employment-related and JOBS-related child care services, transitional child care services, at-risk low income child care services or child care and development block grant services, are disregarded. 18 NYCRR 360-4.6(a)(1)(xxiv); Medicaid Reference Guide, at 221.

CRIME VICTIMS ASSISTANCE:

Payments received from a fund established by a state to aid victims of crime are disregarded. 18 NYCRR 360-4.6(a)(2)(xx); 92 ADM-32, at 3 and 5; Medicaid Reference Guide, at 222.

DISASTER ASSISTANCE:

Any federal major disaster and emergency assistance provided under the Disaster Relief Act of 1974 (P.L. 93-288), as amended by the Disaster Relief and Emergency Assistance Amendments of 1988 (P.L. 100-707), and any comparable disaster assistance provided by states, local governments, and disaster assistance organizations, are disregarded. 18 NYCRR 360-4.6(a)(1)(xxvi); Medicaid Reference Guide, at 222.

DIVIDENDS AND INTEREST:

Page 224 of the Medicaid Reference Guide states that dividends and interest from most resources are disregarded, but the Dividend and Interest portion of the Income section should be referred to for a list of resources which generate interest/dividend income that is countable for SSI-related applicants/recipients.

Page 130 of the Medicaid Reference Guide is the Dividend and Interest portion of the Income section of the book. It states that dividends and interest are included with other sources of income, except for SSI-Related applicants/recipients under community budgeting. Page 133 of the Medicaid Reference Guide states that this exclusion is just for community budgeting, not chronic care budgeting.

Does this mean that dividends and interest are countable for SSI-Related applicants/recipients under chronic care budgeting?

Page 132 states that interest or dividends from most sources is disregarded for SSI-related A/Rs. It lists a few types of resources and states when interest or dividends generated them is countable. This conflicts with page 133, unless the list is just for SSI-Related people under community budgeting. The list includes:

- Retroactive SSI and RSDI (Retirement, Survivors and Disability payments) for 9 months following the month of receipt.

- Unspent state or local government relocation payments for 9 months following the month of receipt. This does not include federal or federally assisted funds.

- Unspent tax refunds related to an earned income tax credit or child tax credit, for the second through ninth months following receipt.

- Unspent state crime victims compensation payments, for nine months following the month of receipt.

DONATED FOOD:

The value of federally donated food is disregarded. 18 NYCRR 360-4.6(a)(1)(ix); Medicaid Reference Guide, at 223.

EARNED INCOME TAX CREDIT:

Refunds or advance payments of the Federal Earned Income Tax Credit are disregarded. 18 NYCRR 360-4.6(a)(1)(xxiii); 92 ADM-32, at 6; Medicaid Reference Guide, at 223.

ECONOMIC OPPORTUNITY ACT LOANS:

Any loan made to a family under Title III of the Federal Economic Opportunity Act is disregarded. 18 NYCRR 360-4.6(a)(1)(ii); Medicaid Reference Guide, at 228.

EDUCATION EXPENSES:

Any portion of a grant, scholarship or fellowship used for tuition, fees, or other necessary educational expenses (excluding general living expenses) is disregarded. 18 NYCRR 360-4.6(a)(1)(xviii); Medicaid Reference Guide, at 227.

Student loans received by an undergraduate or graduate student are disregarded. Medicaid Reference Guide, at 228.

EARNED INCOME -- SIXTY-FIVE DOLLARS PER MONTH:

The first $65 per month of earned income is disregarded. 18 NYCRR 360-4.6(a)(2)(iv); Medicaid Reference Guide, at 223.

EARNED INCOME -- ONE-HALF OF REMAINING:

One-half of the remaining earned income after the disregards from 18 NYCRR 360-4.6 (a) through (d) are disregarded. 18 NYCRR 360-4.6(a)(2)(vi).

EMPLOYMENT EXPENSES:

Payments made to compensate for expenses incident to employment under subparagraph (xi) or (xii) of this paragraph are disregarded. 18 NYCRR 360-4.6(a)(1)(xiii).

ENERGY ASSISTANCE:

Federal energy assistance payments are disregarded. 18 NYCRR 360-4.6(a)(1)(iii); Medicaid Reference Guide, at 223.

EXPENSES OF OBTAINING INCOME:

The portion of a payment that is an essential expense incurred in receiving the payment is disregarded, such as legal fees and other expenses connected with a claim. Medicaid Reference Guide, at 223.

FOOD STAMPS:

The value of food stamp coupons is disregarded. 18 NYCRR 360-4.6(a)(1)(viii); Medicaid Reference Guide, at 223.

FOSTER CARE:

Payments received by foster parents for care of foster children are disregarded. 18 NYCRR 360-4.6(a)(1)(iv); Medicaid Reference Guide, at 223.

FREE MEALS:

The value of free school lunches is disregarded. 18 NYCRR 360-4.6(a)(1)(vi); Medicaid Reference Guide, at 228. The value of other free meals is disregarded, except when more than one meal per day is furnished or when the applicant receives an allowance for meals away from home. 18 NYCRR 360-4.6(a)(1)(vii); Medicaid Reference Guide, at 224.

GARDEN PRODUCE & LIVESTOCK:

The value of garden produce or livestock when used solely by the applicant/recipient and dependents is disregarded. 18 NYCRR 360-4.6(a)(1)(v); Medicaid Reference Guide, at 224.

GI BILL:

The portion of a military person's pay which is deducted by mandate to help fund the GI Bill is disregarded. Medicaid Reference Guide, at 224.

HOME ENERGY ASSISTANCE PAYMENTS:

Home energy assistance payments which are based on financial need are disregarded. 18 NYCRR 360-4.6(a)(2)(xvi).

HOSTILE FIRE PAY:

Income received from hostile fire pay under U.S.C. Title 37 section 310 received while in active military service is disregarded. 18 NYCRR 360-4.6(a)(2)(xxiii); Medicaid Reference Guide, at 224.

HUD COMMUNITY BLOCK GRANTS:

Any funds received by an applicant from the Department of Housing and Urban Development community block grants are disregarded. 18

NYCRR 360-4.6(a)(1)(xv); Medicaid Reference Guide, at 224.

INCOME DISREGARDED ELSEWHERE:

Any other income that a federal law or regulation requires to be disregarded is disregarded. 18 NYCRR 360-4.6(a)(1)(xxix); Medicaid Reference Guide, at 225.

INFREQUENTLY/IRREGULARLY RECEIVED INCOME:

Infrequently or irregularly received income up to $20 of unearned income per month and $10 of earned income per month is disregarded. 18 NYCRR 360-4.6(a)(2)(x). Note that GIS 04 MA/030, at 1, and Medicaid Reference Guide, at 224, state $60 unearned and $30 earned.

INSURANCE PAYMENTS:

Insurance payments are disregarded if they are paid directly to a third party, such as a loan company or a bank to cover loan payments or installment payments in case of death or disability. An example of this would be mortgage insurance. Medicaid Reference Guide, at 228.

LOANS:

Bona fide loans, as described in section 352.22 of this Title, are disregarded. 18 NYCRR 360-4.6(a)(1)(xxv); Medicaid Reference Guide, at 221.

NATIVE AMERICAN PAYMENTS:

Distributions to Native Americans of funds appropriated in satisfaction of judgments of the Indian Claims Commission or the United States Court of Federal Claims are disregarded. 18 NYCRR 360-4.6(a)(1)(xxvii); Medicaid Reference Guide, at 225. Seneca Nation

Settlement Act payments made under PL 101-503 to the Seneca Nation are disregarded. Medicaid Reference Guide, at 225.

Up to $2,000 per year of income from interests of the individual Native Americans in trust or restricted lands, from funds appropriated in satisfaction of judgments of the Indian Claims Commission or United States Court of Federal Claims, is disregarded. 18 NYCRR 360-4.6(a)(1)(xxviii); Medicaid Reference Guide, at 225.

The following Alaskan Native Claims Settlement (ANSCA) distributions are disregarded: cash, up to $2,000 per person per year; stock; a partnership interest; land; an interest in land; an interest in a settlement trust. Medicaid Reference Guide, at 225.

NEED-BASED ASSISTANCE:

Regular cash assistance payments based on need and furnished as supplemental income by the federal government, a state or political subdivision are disregarded. 18 NYCRR 360-4.6(a)(1)(xix); Medicaid Reference Guide, at 220 and 221.

Support and maintenance assistance based on need provided in-kind by a private non-profit agency are disregarded. Support and maintenance assistance based on need provided in cash or in-kind also are disregarded if provided by: a supplier of home heating oil or gas, an entity whose revenues are primarily derived on a rate-of-return basis regulated by the State or Federal governmental entity or a municipal utility providing home energy. Medicaid Reference Guide, at 220.

Money paid by a third party directly to a vendor is disregarded, unless it is for food, clothing and shelter. Medicaid Reference Guide, at 220.

NONMEDICAL IMPAIRMENT-RELATED WORK EXPENSES:

For disabled Medicaid recipients, nonmedical impairment-related work expenses are disregarded. 18 NYCRR 360-4.6(a)(2)(v); Medicaid Reference Guide, at 224.

OLDER AMERICANS ACT ASSISTANCE:

Any assistance to an individual (other than wages or salaries) under the Federal Older Americans Act of 1965 is disregarded. 18 NYCRR 360-4.6(a)(2)(xviii); Medicaid Reference Guide, at 223.

OVERPAYMENTS:

Withholding to recover a previous overpayment is disregarded if the person received Medicaid at the time the overpayment was made, and the overpayment amount was included in determining his Medicaid eligibility. Medicaid Reference Guide, at 225.

PREVENTATIVE HOUSING PAYMENTS:

Payments provided as a preventative housing service under section 423.4(1) of this Title are disregarded. 18 NYCRR 360-4.6(a)(1)(xx); Medicaid Reference Guide, at 226.

RADIATION EXPOSURE COMPENSATION TRUST FUND PAYMENTS:

Payments for injuries or deaths resulting from exposure to radiation from nuclear testing and uranium mining are disregarded. Medicaid Reference Guide, at 226.

RELOCATION ASSISTANCE:

Any federal payment received under Title II of the Uniform Relocation Assistance and Real Property Acquisition Policies Act of 1970 is disregarded. 18 NYCRR 360-4.6(a)(1)(i); Medicaid Reference Guide, at 223. Relocation assistance received on or after 05/01/1991 that is provided by a state or local government and is comparable to assistance provided under Title II of the Uniform Relocation Assistance and Real Property Acquisitions Policies Act of 1970 which is subject to the treatment required by section 216 of the Act is disregarded. 18

NYCRR 360-4.6(a)(2)(xxi); Medicaid Reference Guide, at 227. Interest and dividends generated from unspent state or local government relocation assistance payments (not federal or federally assisted funds) for 9 months after receipt are disregarded. Medicaid Reference Guide, at 226.

RENTAL INCOME EXPENSES:

The following rental income expenses are disregarded:
(1)   Property, school, water and sewer taxes
(2)   Utilities, if they are included in the rent
(3)   Fire, windstorm, flood, theft and liability insurance
(4)   Interest payments on mortgages for the property
(5)   Cost of essential repairs, but not improvements
(6)   Wages paid to employees for maintaining the property
(7)   Advertising for tenants
(8)   Other expenses essential to maintaining the property, such as lawn care and snow removal. Medicaid Reference Guide, at 144-45.
(9)   If the rental property is also the homestead, such as a two-family residence, the allowable expenses are prorated based on the number of units designated for rent. 18 NYCRR 360-4.3 (d)(1); Medicaid Reference Guide, at 145.

See page 145 of the Medicaid Reference Guide for examples of expenses which are not deductible.

If a person rents out part of his homestead, he can deduct the rental expenses listed above to the extent that they are attributable to the rental portion of the property. 18 NYCRR 360-4.3 (d)(2).

REPARATION PAYMENTS

JAPANESE-AMERICAN & ALEUTS: Benefits paid to eligible Japanese-American or Aleuts under the Federal Civil Liberties Act of 1988 and the Aleutian and Pribilof Islands Restitution Act are disregarded. 18 NYCRR 360-4.6(a)(1)(xxi); 91 ADM-8; Medicaid Reference Guide, at 225.

GERMAN REPARATION PAYMENTS: All reparation payments received from the Federal Republic of Germany are disregarded. 18 NYCRR 360-4.6(a)(2)(ii); Medicaid Reference Guide, at 225.

AUSTRIAN REPARATION PAYMENTS: Payments made by the Austrian government under paragraphs 500 to 506 of the Austrian General Social Insurance Act, if the payments remain identifiable as such, are disregarded. 18 NYCRR 360-4.6(a)(2)(xxii); 92 ADM-32, at 4 and 6; Medicaid Reference Guide, at 225-26.

NETHERLANDS REPARATION PAYMENTS: Payments based on Nazi persecution, but not Japanese persecution, are disregarded. Medicaid Reference Guide, at 226.

REPLACEMENT OF ASSISTANCE ALREADY PAID:

Replacement of assistance already paid, such as a lost or stolen check, is disregarded. Medicaid Reference Guide, at 227.

SSI:

SSI payments received by the applicant/recipient are disregarded. Medicaid Reference Guide, at 228.

SSI, RETROACTIVE:

Retroactive benefits under the SSI program are disregarded. 18 NYCRR 360-4.6(a)(2)(xix); Medicaid Reference Guide, at 227.

SUPPORT & MAINTENANCE BASED ON NEED:

Any support and maintenance provided based on need according to section 352.22(s) of this Title are disregarded. 18 NYCRR 360-4.6(a)(1)(xvi); Medicaid Reference Guide, at 220.

TAX REFUNDS FROM REAL ESTATE OR FOOD PURCHASES:

Any refund received from a public agency of taxes paid on real estate or food purchases is disregarded. 18 NYCRR 360-4.6(a)(2)(ix); Medicaid Reference Guide, at 226.

UNEARNED INCOME -- TWENTY DOLLARS PER MONTH

The first $20 per month of unearned income per couple is disregarded. 18 NYCRR 360-4.6(a)(2) (iii); Medicaid Reference Guide, at 228.

VETERANS ADMINISTRATION REDUCED PENSION:

Reduced (limited) $90 Veterans Administration pension payments are disregarded. Medicaid Reference Guide, at 226.

VETERANS' AID & ATTENDANCE AND UNUSUAL MEDICAL EXPENSES:

Aid and attendance benefits and household benefits received from the Veterans' Administration are disregarded. 18 NYCRR 360-4.6(a)(2)(viii); Medicaid Reference Guide, at 229. Payments to veterans for Unusual Medical Expenses also are disregarded. Medicaid Reference Guide, at 229.

VOCATIONAL REHABILITATION ACT PAYMENTS:

Any payments made under the Federal Vocational Rehabilitation Act are disregarded. 18 NYCRR 360-4.6(a)(2)(xiii); Medicaid Reference Guide, at 229.

VOLUNTEER PAYMENTS:

RSVP: Payments made to participants in the Retired Senior Volunteer Program under the Domestic Volunteer Services Act for services provided to adults who have exceptional needs is disregarded. 18 NYCRR 360-4.6(a)(1)(xi); Medicaid Reference Guide, at 229.

Foster Grandparents: Payments made to participants in the Foster Grandparent Program under the Domestic Volunteer Services Act are disregarded. 18 NYCRR 360-4.6(a)(1)(xii); Medicaid Reference Guide, at 229.

VISTA: Payments made to volunteers under the VISTA program are disregarded. 18 NYCRR 360-4.6(a)(1)(xiv); Medicaid Reference Guide, at 220 and 229.

Senior Companions Program: Payments made to volunteers under the Senior Companion Program of the Domestic Volunteer Services Act are disregarded. Medicaid Reference Guide, at 229.

Senior Health Aide Program: Payments made to volunteers under the Senior Health Aide Program of the Domestic Volunteer Services Act are disregarded. Medicaid Reference Guide, at 229.

SCORE: Payments made to volunteers under the Service Corps of Retired Executives program established under Title III of P.L. 93-133 are disregarded. Medicaid Reference Guide, at 229.

ACE: Payments made to volunteers under the Active Corps of Executives program established under Title III of P.L. 93-133 are disregarded. Medicaid Reference Guide, at 229.

WIC BENEFITS:

The value of WIC benefits is disregarded. 18 NYCRR 360-4.6(a)(1)(x); Medicaid Reference Guide, at 229.

INCOME -- AFTER MONTH ONE -- PERSON IN A NURSING HOME WHO DOES NOT HAVE A COMMUNITY SPOUSE

After the first month in the nursing home, if an applicant does not have a community spouse, most of his income will go to the nursing home. He will be allowed to keep a Personal Needs Allowance. If he has health insurance, he will be allowed to keep enough income to cover the cost of the premiums. Some types of income are disregarded. He will have to pay the rest of his income to the nursing home each month.

PERSONAL NEEDS ALLOWANCE:

If the applicant does not have a community spouse, he is allowed to keep a Personal Needs Allowance (PNA) each month, after the first month in the nursing home. 18 NYCRR 360-4.9 (a)(1).

A personal needs allowance is the amount set aside to meet the personal needs of a person who is in permanent absence status in a medical institution. Medicaid Reference Guide, glossary xvi.

For many years, the Personal Needs Allowance has been $50 per month. Social Services Law section 366 (2)(a)(10)(ii)(A); 18 NYCRR 360-4.9(a)(1); Medicaid Reference Guide, at 280 and 288.

For 2008, GIS 07 MA/025 listed the Medicaid Only Income Exemption and Resource Levels. It stated that the applicant could keep $50 per month of income. In more recent years, the GISs which listed the Medicaid income and resource levels have not included a Personal Needs Allowance amount. See GIS 08 MA/035, GIS 09 MA/026 and GIS 10 MA/026.

Attachment 2 of 09-INF-14, Personal Needs Allowance (PNA) in Non-Medical Facilities and Medical Facilities Desk Aid, dated 06/25/2009, shows a Personal Needs Allowance of $50 per month for a Medicaid-only recipient in permanent absent status in a nursing home, effective January 1, 2009.

HEALTH INSURANCE PREMIUMS:

The applicant is allowed to keep enough income to cover the cost of health insurance premiums. 18 NYCRR 360-4.9 (a)(2). Health insurance premiums are discussed elsewhere in this book.

INCOME DISREGARDS AFTER MONTH ONE:

After the first month in the nursing home, some types of income are disregarded, but not as many as during the first month.

After the first month in the nursing home, the income disregards for Medicaid recipients in any category and the SSI-related income disregards do not apply. 18 NYCRR 360-4.9; Medicaid Reference Guide, at 280 and 288.

After the first month, the following types of income are disregarded for the applicant:

Money received from a lawsuit against the nursing home for improper and/or inadequate treatment is disregarded. 18 NYCRR 360-4.9 (a)(5)(i).

Income necessary to achieve a plan of self-support under 18 NYCRR 360-4.6(a)(2)(xx) is disregarded. 18 NYCRR 360-4.9 (a)(5)(ii).

SSI benefits are disregarded. 18 NYCRR 360-4.9(a)(5)(iii).

Federal Republic of Germany reparation payments are disregarded. 18 NYCRR 360-4.9 (a)(5)(iv).

Payments to Japanese-Americans and Aleuts under the Federal Civil Liberties Act of 1988 and the Aleutian and Pribilof Islands Restitution Act are disregarded. 18 NYCRR 360-4.9 (a)(5)(v); 91 ADM-8.

Payments from the Agent Orange Settlement Fund or any other fund established in the In re Agent Orange product liability litigation settlement, and payments from court proceedings for personal injuries sustained by veterans from exposure to dioxin or phenoxy herbicides in the war in Indochina between 01/01/1963 and 05/07/1975 are disregarded. 18 NYCRR 360-4.9 (a)(5)(vi); 91 ADM-8.

Note that Veteran's surviving spouse reduced pension payments do count towards the Personal Needs Allowance. 18 NYCRR 360-4.9 (a)(5)(vii).

INCOME -- AFTER MONTH ONE -- PERSON IN A NURSING HOME WHO DOES HAVE A COMMUNITY SPOUSE

After the first month in the nursing home, if an applicant does have a community spouse, he will be allowed to keep a Personal Needs Allowance. If he has health insurance, he will be allowed to keep enough income to cover the cost of the premiums. Some types of income are disregarded. If the community spouse's own income is below the level of what she is allowed to keep, then the applicant will be allowed to keep extra income to give to her. The applicant will have to pay the rest of his income to the nursing home each month.

PERSONAL NEEDS ALLOWANCE:

18 NYCRR 360-4.9 (b) states that an applicant who has a community spouse can keep the items in 18 NYCRR 360-4.10 (b)(4).

18 NYCRR 360-4.10 (b)(4)(i) is a personal needs allowance. See also 42 U.S.C. section 1396r-5 (d)(1)(A).

A personal needs allowance is the amount set aside to meet the personal needs of a person who is in permanent absence status in a medical institution. Medicaid Reference Guide, glossary xvi.

For many years, the PNA has been $50 per month. Social Services Law section 366 (2)(a)(10)(ii)(A); 18 NYCRR 360-4.9(a)(1); Medicaid Reference Guide, at 280 and 288.

For 2008, GIS 07 MA/025 spelled out the Medicaid Only Income Exemption and Resource Levels. It stated that the person in the nursing home could keep $50 per month of income. In more recent years, the GISs which listed the Medicaid income and resource levels have not included a Personal Needs Allowance amount. See GIS 08 MA/035, GIS 09 MA/026 and GIS 10 MA/026.

Attachment 2 of 09-INF-14, dated 06/25/2009, shows a Personal Needs Allowance of $50 per month for a Medicaid-only recipient in permanent absent status in a nursing home, effective January 1, 2009.

HEALTH INSURANCE PREMIUMS:

18 NYCRR 360-4.9 (b) states that an applicant who has a community spouse can keep all of the same items listed in 18 NYCRR 360-4.9 (a)(2) that a person without a community spouse can keep.

18 NYCRR 360-4.9 (a)(2) is a deduction for health insurance premiums.

INCOME DISREGARDS AFTER MONTH ONE:

18 NYCRR 360-4.9 (b) also states that an applicant who has a community spouse can keep all of the same items listed in 18 NYCRR 360-4.9 (a)(5) that a person without a community spouse can keep.

18 NYCRR 360-4.9 (a)(5) items are:

Money received from a lawsuit against the nursing home for improper and/or inadequate treatment. 18 NYCRR 360-4.9 (a)(5)(i).

Income necessary to achieve a plan of self-support under 18 NYCRR 360-4.6(a)(2)(xx). 18 NYCRR 360-4.9 (a)(5)(ii).

SSI benefits. 18 NYCRR 360-4.9(a)(5)(iii).

Federal Republic of Germany reparation payments. 18 NYCRR 360-4.9 (a)(5)(iv).

Payments to Japanese-Americans and Aleuts under the Federal Civil Liberties Act of 1988 and the Aleutian and Pribilof Islands Restitution Act. 18 NYCRR 360-4.9 (a)(5)(v); 91 ADM-8.

Agent Orange Payments. Payments from the Agent Orange Settlement Fund or any other fund established in the In re Agent Orange product liability litigation settlement, and payments from court proceedings for personal injuries sustained by veterans from exposure to dioxin or phenoxy herbicides in the war in Indochina between 01/01/1963 and

05/07/1975. 18 NYCRR 360-4.9 (a)(5)(vi).

After the first month in the nursing home, the income disregards for Medicaid recipients in any category and the SSI-related income disregards do not apply. 18 NYCRR 360-4.9; Medicaid Reference Guide, at 280 and 288. Thus, the applicant would be limited to the income disregards described above.

Note that veteran's surviving spouse reduced pension payments do count towards the Personal Needs Allowance. 18 NYCRR 360-4.9 (a)(5)(vii).

PAYMENTS TO THE COMMUNITY SPOUSE:

18 NYCRR 360-4.10 (b)(4)(ii) is a community spouse monthly income allowance, which would be paid to the community spouse whose income is below the MMMNA. See also 42 U.S.C. 1396r-5 (d)(1)(B). The community spouse monthly income allowance is discussed elsewhere in this book.

HEALTH INSURANCE PREMIUMS

If the applicant has health insurance, the Department of Social Services usually has him keep his health insurance, and allows him to keep enough income each month to pay the health insurance premiums. N.Y. Social Services Law section 366 (2)(a)(6); 18 NYCRR 360-4.6(a)(2)(vii); 18 NYCRR 360-4.9 (a)(2); Medicaid Reference Guide, at 224, 239 and 288.

The Department of Social Services usually finds it cost-effective to allow the Medicaid recipient to keep his health insurance. Generally, Medicare pays medical bills first, and the health insurance pays second. Medicaid only has to pay whatever is left. Medicaid is a payer of last resort. 18 NYCRR 360-7.2 and 18 NYCRR 360-7.3(b)(2)(i); Medicaid Reference Guide at 423.

If the Department of Social Service required the Medicaid recipient to cancel his health insurance, then Medicaid would move up to the second spot when there are medical bills to pay, rather than being in the third spot.

A Medicaid recipient must use health, hospital or accident insurance benefits to the fullest extent. 18 NYCRR 360-7.3 (b).

If the Medicaid recipient pays his health insurance premiums and this drops his income below the level he is allowed to keep, the Department of Social Services must pay or reimburse him for the cost of the premium, if the premium is cost-effective. GIS 02 MA/019 and GIS 06 MA/026. The payment or reimbursement cannot be more than the difference between his net available income and the appropriate income level. GIS 02 MA/019; GIS 06 MA/026.

If the Medicaid recipient is below the resource level, the Department of Social Services might reimburse him for the cost of his health insurance premiums, including the cost of his Medicare A premium. Medicaid Reference Guide at 213, 240 and 428.

If the Medicaid recipient has a community spouse, and the community spouse is taking a community spouse monthly income allowance from him because the community spouse is below the MMMNA, the

Department of Social Services might reimburse the community spouse for the cost of health insurance premiums of the Medicaid recipient. They might do this even if the community spouse exercised spousal refusal.

If the Medicaid recipient has not paid his health insurance premiums, and he is at risk of losing his health insurance, the Department of Social Services might pay those premiums for him. Medicaid Reference Guide, at 428.

If the Medicaid recipient is paying for prescription drug insurance, the Department of Social Services usually will not allow him to keep that insurance. If someone is eligible for Medicare and Medicaid, they must go on Medicare D for payment of prescription drugs, unless doing so will result in them losing cost-effective health insurance. GIS 05 MA/024, at 1; GIS 06 MA/003, at 1; Medicaid Reference Guide, at 415. However, that waiver will not be allowed if the Medicaid recipient has a legally responsible relative who refuses to provide medical support. GIS 06 MA/003, at 1.

There are no co-pays for Medicare D for people in nursing homes. 05 OMM/ADM-5, at 4; Medicaid Reference Guide, at 416. There are no deductibles. 05 OMM/ADm-5, at 4.

The Centers for Medicare and Medicaid Services (CMS) selects a Medicare D plan for the person in the nursing home; he can choose a different plan if he likes. 05 OMM/ADM-5, at 5.

COMMUNITY SPOUSE'S INCOME

THE MMMNA:

The community spouse is allowed to keep a certain amount of income each month. This is referred to as the Minimum Monthly Maintenance Needs Allowance (MMMNA). Social Services Law section 366-c (2)(h); 18 NYCRR 360-4.10(a)(8); Medicaid Reference Guide, at 276.

The community spouse is allowed to keep $2,739 per month of income during 2011. GIS 10 MA/026. This is the same figure as 2010 and 2009.

HEALTH INSURANCE PREMIUMS:

If the community spouse has health insurance, the Department of Social Services usually lets her keep the health insurance, and allows her to keep enough income each month (in addition to the MMMNA) to pay the health insurance premiums. 89 ADM-47, at 17; Medicaid Reference Guide, at 276; 42 U.S.C. 1396r-5 (d)(2).

INCOME DISREGARDS FOR THE COMMUNITY SPOUSE:

A few types of income are disregarded for the community spouse:

Austrian and German reparation payments. GIS 97 MA/018; Medicaid Reference Guide, at 276.

Netherlands reparation payments. Medicaid Reference Guide, at 276.

Benefits paid to Japanese-Americans and Aleuts under the Federal Civil Liberties Act of 1988 and the Aleutian and Pribilof Islands Restitution. GIS 97 MA/018; 91 ADM-8.

Payments made from the Agent Orange Settlement Fund or any other fund established under the settlement in the In Re Agent Orange product liability litigation, and payments received from the court proceedings brought for personal injuries sustained by veterans resulting from exposure to dioxin or phenoxy herbicides in connection with the war in Indochina from 01/01/1962 to 05/07/1975 are disregarded. GIS 97 MA/018.

Self-employment income and rental property income disregards. Medicaid Reference Guide, at 276. See also Medicaid Reference Guide, at 144-45.

COMMUNITY SPOUSE WITH INCOME OVER THE LIMIT:

INCOME CONTRIBUTION TO THE NURSING HOME:

If the community spouse has more than the MMMNA: "The community spouse will be requested to contribute 25 percent of his/her income in excess of the minimum monthly maintenance needs allowance and any family allowances toward the cost of necessary care or assistance for the institutionalized spouse."18 NYCRR 360-4.10(b)(5); 90 INF-19, page 3 of the attachment; 89 ADM-47, at 6 and 20; Medicaid Reference Guide, at 276.

REFUSAL TO MAKE THE INCOME CONTRIBUTION:

"An institutionalized spouse will not be denied MA [Medical Assistance] because the community spouse refuses or fails to make such income available. However, nothing contained in this paragraph prohibits a social services district from enforcing the provisions of the Social Services Law which require financial contributions from legally responsible relatives, or recovering from the community spouse the cost of any MA provided to the institutionalized spouse." 18 NYCRR 360-4.10(b)(5); 90 INF-19, page 3 of the attachment; 89 ADM-47, at 6 and 20; Medicaid Reference Guide, at 276.

Medicaid will not be denied to the applicant because the community spouse refuses to make her income available to meet the cost of his care. However, the Department of Social Services may seek to recover the cost of Medicaid provided from the community spouse, as per N.Y. Social Services Law section 366 (3)(a). 89 ADM-47, at 20.

COMMUNITY SPOUSE WITH INCOME UNDER THE LIMIT:

If the community spouse's income is less than the MMMNA: the institutionalized spouse can give the community spouse enough of his income to bring her up to the MMMNA. 89 ADM-47, at 16-17; Medicaid Reference Guide, at 276. This amount is referred to as the "community spouse monthly income allowance." N.Y. Social Services Law section 366-c (2)(g); Social Services Law section 366-c (4)(b); 18 NYCRR 360-4.10(a)(3) and 18 NYCRR 360-4.10(b)(4)(ii); 91 ADM-33, at 3 and 4; Medicaid Reference Guide, glossary at iv.

There was concern that federal law prohibited the Department of Social Services from requiring the institutionalized spouse to give Social Security income to the community spouse. If the institutionalized spouse did not intend to make this income available to the community spouse, then the community spouse could request a fair hearing or court order to increase the Community Spouse Resource Allowance (CSRA), so that she would have extra resources which would generate enough income to reach the MMMNA. Policy was changed to prevent the community spouse from getting an increased CSRA for this purpose. For a discussion of this issue, see 06 OMM/ADM-3.

If the community spouse has less than the MMMNA, the institutionalized spouse can give her the community spouse monthly income allowance even if she exercised spousal refusal and is keeping all of her resources. Medicaid Reference Guide, at 396.

COMMUNITY SPOUSE WHO WANTS TO KEEP MORE INCOME THAN THE LIMIT:

The community spouse can request a fair hearing or court order allowing her to keep more income than the MMMNA if there are exceptional circumstances resulting in significant financial distress. N.Y. Social Services Law 366-c (8)(b); 18 NYCRR 360-4.10 (b)(6); 89 ADM-47, at 24. Such expenses may be of a recurring nature or one-time costs. They may include, but are not limited to, recurring or extraordinary non-covered medical expenses of the community spouse or family members; amounts to preserve, maintain or make major repairs to the homestead; and amounts needed to preserve an income-producing asset. These are expenses which the community spouse cannot be expected to meet from the MMMNA or the CSRA. 18 NYCRR 360-4.10 (a)(10); 06 OMM/ADM-3, at 6; 89 ADM-47, at 24; 42 U.S.C. 1396r-5 (e)(2)(B).

For a discussion of "exceptional circumstances" and "significant financial distress," see In re Balzarini v. Suffolk County Dept. of Social Services, slip op. 1048 (Court of Appeals of N.Y. 2011).

COMMUNITY SPOUSE WHO WANTS TO KEEP EXTRA RESOURCES TO GENERATE MORE INCOME:

The community spouse can ask to keep more resources than the Community Spouse Resource Allowance (CSRA) if the CSRA does not generate enough income to give the community spouse the MMMNA. N.Y. Social Services Law section 366-c (8)(c); 18 NYCRR 360-4.10 (c)(7); 89 ADM-47, at 23; Medicaid Reference Guide, at 396; 42 U.S.C. section 1396r-5 (e)(2)(C).

Page 3 of 07 OHIP/INF-3 states that when determining how much in resources is needed to generate enough income to bring the community spouse up to the MMMNA, the calculation may be based on the average interest that a savings account generates. As an alternative, fair hearing officers and the Department of Social Services may consider the resource amount needed to purchase a single premium life annuity that would generate the amount needed to bring the community spouse up to the MMMNA. 07 OHIP/INF-3, at 3. Departments of Social Services should advocate for the method that is most cost-effective for the Medicaid program. 07 OHIP/INF-3, at 3. The annuity will have a higher rate of return, but the community spouse's excess resources might not be enough to purchase an annuity, due to minimum investment requirements; in those cases, the savings account interest calculation may be required to be used. 07 OHIP/INF-3, at 4. See 07 OHIP/INF-3, at 3, for examples. Annuity costs can be obtained from a life insurance company, a mutual fund company, or a bank which sells annuities, or from an annuity calculator such as the one at www.immediateannuities.com. 07 OHIP/INF-3, at 4. If the Department of Social Services believes that the purchase of an annuity is most cost-effective for the Medicaid program, then at the fair hearing the

Department of Social Services should show that the annuity would be purchased with a single-time premium, have a fixed rate of return beginning immediately, be actuarially sound, make equal monthly payments for life, not have balloon payments, and have payments terminate when the community spouse dies. 07 OHIP/INF-3, at 4-5. The community spouse does not have to actually purchase an annuity, but the Department of Social Services will budget as though the annuity income was received. 07 OHIP/INF-3, at 6. If an increased CSRA is authorized and the community spouse does purchase an annuity, the State does not have to be named as remainder beneficiary. 07 OHIP/INF-3, at 6. If the community spouse's total income, including income from the annuity, will be more than the MMMNA, the community spouse may be asked to contribute 25% of the excess toward the cost of care of the institutionalized spouse. 07 OHIP/INF-3, at 5.

If the community spouse's income is below the MMMNA, the community spouse cannot be allowed to keep extra resources to generate more income unless the Department of Social Services has already considered the income which the institutionalized spouse could make available to the community spouse. This is the "income first" rule. 89 ADM-47, at 23; Medicaid Reference Guide, at 396; 42 U.S.C. 1396r-5(d)(6).

MEDICAID RULES FOR LONG-TERM CARE INSURANCE POLICIES ISSUED UNDER THE NEW YORK STATE PARTNERSHIP FOR LONG-TERM CARE

Some people purchase long-term care insurance policies which are issued under the New York State Partnership for Long-Term Care. These policies have a Medicaid component, and have special rules under New York's Medicaid program. Note that some long-term care insurance policies are not Partnership policies. See Medicaid Reference Guide, at glossary xiv.

The New York State Partnership for Long-term Care issues several different types of long-term care insurance policies. They are described at the home page of the New York State Partnership for Long-Term Care, which is www.nyspltc.org.

When the owner of a Partnership policy has used up his benefits under the policy, he can go on Medicaid. This is referred to as "Medicaid Extended Coverage." 09 OHIP/ADM-3, at 3; Medicaid Reference Guide, at glossary xii and 430. Medicaid Extended Coverage will be retroactive to the first day of the month in which the minimum duration requirements under the policy were met. 09 OHIP/ADM-3, at 21.

When the owner goes on Medicaid, some or all of his resources will be exempt, depending on the type of Partnership policy he had. 09 OHIP/ADM-3.

When the owner goes on Medicaid, the Medicaid income rules apply. 09 OHIP/ADM-3, at 3; Medicaid Reference Guide, at 430.1 and glossary page xii. The Medicaid income rules are discussed elsewhere in this book.

GIS 10 MA/016, citing Social Services Law section 367-f, states that if the owner is subject to SSI-Related community budgeting and he is married, he is entitled to a monthly income level equal to the spousal impoverishment minimum monthly maintenance needs allowance. If the owner is subject to SSI-Related community budgeting and he is single, he is entitled to a monthly income level equal to one-half of the minimum monthly maintenance needs allowance. If he has more income than that, he can spend down to the new level; he does not need to spend down to the Medicaid level. The GIS states that these income levels do not affect post-eligibility treatment of income for an applicant/recipient who is subject to chronic care budgeting. See also Medicaid Reference Guide, at 430-31.

Social Services Law section 367-f (1)(a) states that Medicaid eligibility will be based "on an income eligibility standard for married couples equal to the amount of the minimum monthly maintenance needs allowance defined in paragraph (h) of subdivision two of section three hundred sixty-six-c of this title, and for single individuals equal to one-half of such amount."

When the owner goes on Medicaid, he can be required to pursue, or cooperate in the pursuit of, income payments to which he is entitled, such as the failure of a trustee to make required income distributions to him. GIS 01 MA/022, at 1; 09 OHIP/ADM-3, at 16.

Medicaid does not require the pursuit of income if it would reduce the value of the resource which generates the income. GIS 01/MA 022, at 2; 09 OHIP/ADM-3, at 16.

The owner cannot be required to take periodic payments from an annuity. GIS 01 MA/022, at 2; 09 OHIP/ADM-3, at 16.

The owner cannot be required to maximize payments from an annuity if that would reduce the annuity's value. GIS 01 MA/022, at 2. However, if the interest can be withdrawn, the owner must pursue it. GIS 01 MA/022, at 2; 09 OHIP/ADM-3, at 16.

The owner cannot be required to maximize income from a retirement fund. GIS 98 MA/024, at 2; 09 OHIP/ADM-3, at 16.

If the owner or his spouse transfers income, there may be a Medicaid penalty period, even if there would not have been a penalty period for the transfer of resources. GIS 01 MA/022, at 1; 09 OHIP/ADM-3, at 9 and 18.

TOTAL ASSET PROTECTION PARTNERSHIP PLANS:

There are two types of Total Asset Protection Partnership plans. See Medicaid Reference Guide, at glossary xxiii.

Total Asset 50 Protection Plan: When the owner of a Total Asset 50 Protection Plan needs long-term care, the policy will pay for three years of care in a nursing home or six years of care at home, or some combination, with two home care days equaling one nursing home day. 09 OHIP/ADM-3, at 5; Medicaid Reference Guide, at 431.

Total Asset 100 Protection Plan: When the owner of a Total Asset 100 Protection Plan needs long-term care, the policy will pay for four years of care in a nursing home or four years of care at home or some combination, with one home care day equaling one nursing home day. 09 OHIP/ADM-3, at 6; Medicaid Reference Guide, at 431-32.

When the owner of a Total Asset Protection Plan has used up the benefits under the policy, he can apply for Medicaid and all of his resources and his spouse's resources will be exempt. 09 OHIP/ADM-3, at 9 and 16. See also Social Services Law section 367-f (1)(a); 96 ADM-8, at 21 (issued before Dollar for Dollar Protection plans were available); Medicaid Reference Guide, at 432.

Since resources are exempt, it is not necessary to provide documentation of them to the Department of Social Services when applying for Medicaid. 09 OHIP/ADM-3, at 9 and 14; Medicaid Reference Guide, at 432.

Since resources are exempt, transfer of resource rules do not apply. 09 OHIP/ADM-3, at 9 and 18. There are no penalty periods for transfer of resources. 96 ADM-8, at 21; GIS 07 MA/020, at 1; Medicaid Reference Guide, at 432.

Income is not exempt, so there can be a penalty period for the transfer of income. Medicaid Reference Guide, at 432.

The owner of a Total Asset Protection Plan must be in New York State when he goes on Medicaid. 09 OHIP/ADM-3, at 7; Medicaid Reference Guide, at 430.

Normally, when a Medicaid applicant is in a nursing home, his homestead is not exempt if his equity interest in it exceeds the limit in the Substantial Home Equity Rule. The Substantial Home Equity Rule is discussed elsewhere in this book. When the owner of a Total Asset Protection Plan has used up his benefits under the policy, the Substantial Home Equity Rule does not apply. 09 OHIP/ADM-3, at 13; GIS 07 MA/007; Medicaid Reference Guide at 401-02 and 432.

When the owner of a Total Asset Protection Plan has used up his benefits under the policy, no lien may be imposed against his real estate. Social Services Law section 367-f (1)(a); 09 OHIP/ADM-3 at 10 and 20; 02 OMM/ADM-3, at 8; Medicaid Reference Guide at 430, 680 and 684.

No recoveries will be pursued against the estate of an owner of a Total Asset Protection Plan. Social Services Law section 367-f (1)(a); 09 OHIP/ADM-3, at 3, 10 and 20; Medicaid Reference Guide at 430, 680 and 684.

When the owner of a Total Asset Protection plan has used up his benefits under the policy, any annuity purchased by him or by his spouse is exempt from Medicaid's annuity requirements. 09 OHIP/ADM-3, at 11-12; GIS 07/MA020, at 1; Medicaid Reference Guide at 432.

DOLLAR FOR DOLLAR PROTECTION PARTNERSHIP PLANS:

Dollar for Dollar Protection Plans were first offered in New York in the year 2005. When reading about Partnership policies, always check the date that the document was written. Anything written before 2005 may have assumed that Partnership policies were limited to Total Asset Protection plans.

There are two types of Dollar for Dollar Protection Partnership plans. See Medicaid Reference Guide, at glossary vi.

Dollar for Dollar 50 Protection Plan: When the owner of a Dollar for Dollar 50 Protection Plan needs long-term care, the policy will pay for 1.5 years of care in a nursing home or three years of care at home, or some combination, with two home care days equaling one nursing home day. 09 OHIP/ADM-3, at 6; Medicaid Reference Guide, at 432.

Dollar for Dollar 100 Protection Plan: When the owner of a Dollar for Dollar 100 Protection Plan needs long-term care, the policy will pay for two years of care in a nursing home or two years of care at home or some combination, with one home care day equaling one nursing home day. 09 OHIP/ADM-3, at 6-7; Medicaid Reference Guide at 432.

When the owner of a Dollar for Dollar Protection plan has used up the benefits under the policy, he can apply for Medicaid. His assets will be protected in an amount equal to the dollar amount of benefits paid out by the policy; the rest of his assets are not protected and are subject to the Medicaid rules. If the owner is married, the spouse's resources are counted to the extent that the couple's combined resources above the community spouse resource allowance exceed the dollar amount of benefits paid out by the policy. 09 OHIP/ADM-3, at 9 and 17. See also Social Services Law section 367-f (1)(a); Medicaid Reference Guide, at 432-33. From the couple's combined countable resources, subtract the following in the order listed: (1) the community spouse resource allowance; (2) the dollar amount paid by the policy; (3) the Medicaid resource level for one. The remainder is excess resources. 09 OHIP/ADM-3, at 17.

09 OHIP/ADM-3 has an example on page 17:

	300,000	couple's total countable resources
-	109,560	Community Spouse Resource Allowance
	190,444	
-	176,000	dollar amount paid by policy
	14,440	
-	13,800	Medicaid resource level for one
	640	excess resources

Since all of the owner's resources are not protected, the owner has to provide the Department of Social Services with documentation of his resources and the community spouse's resources for the length of the look-back period if he applies for Medicaid. 09 OHIP/ADM-3, at 10 and 15.

The owner of a Dollar for Dollar Protection Plan must be in New York

State when he goes on Medicaid. 09 OHIP/ADM-3, at 7; Medicaid Reference Guide, at 430.

When the owner of a Dollar for Dollar Protection Plan has used up his benefits under the policy, the Substantial Home Equity Rule does not apply. 09 OHIP/ADM-3, at 13; GIS 07 MA/007; Medicaid Reference Guide, at 401-02. The Substantial Home Equity Rule is discussed elsewhere in this book.

When the owner of a Dollar for Dollar Protection Plan has used up his benefits under the policy, if real property is disregarded or exempt when determining Medicaid eligibility, and the owner intends to return home, but the home is not occupied by a spouse, minor child, certified blind or certified disabled child, or a sibling with an equity interest has not lived there since at least one year before the owner went in the nursing home, then a lien shall be placed on the homestead to recover the amount by which the fair market value of the property exceeds the amount of the owner's protected amount under the policy. 09 OHIP/ADM-3 at 20; Social Services Law section 367-f (1)(a); Medicaid Reference Guide at 430, 680 and 684.

Estate recovery against the owner of a Dollar for Dollar Protection Plan will be reduced by the amount of assets protected by the policy. Social Services Law section 367-f (1)(a); 09 OHIP/ADM-3, at 20-21; Medicaid Reference Guide, at 430.

When the owner of a Dollar for Dollar Protection Plan has used up his benefits under the policy, a prohibited transfer made within the look-back period must be offset by any remaining dollar-for-dollar disregard that was not used toward the owner's countable resources. There will be a penalty period for the rest of the transfer. 09 OHIP/ADM-3, at 10 and 19; Medicaid Reference Guide, at 433. (Note that 96 ADM-8 was issued before Dollar for Dollar Protection plans were available.)

09 OHIP/ADM-3 has an example on page 19.

	175,000	countable resources
-	200,000	Dollar for Dollar Protection Plan amount
	(25,000)	portion of DDPP amount not needed to cover countable resources

	20,000	gift
-	13,800	Medicaid resource level for one
	6,200	
-	25,000	DDPP amount available to cover the gift
	(18,800)	all of the gift has been covered, so the person is eligible for Medicaid. No penalty period.

One year after the person is approved for Medicaid, he will need to be recertified. At recertification, he cannot use the full $200,000 to cover his resources because he used $6,200 of it to cover a gift.

	200,000	total DDPP protection amount
-	6,200	amount of DDPP protection used to cover the gift
	193,800	amount of DDPP protection which can be used to cover resources at recertification

When the owner of a Dollar for Dollar Protection plan has used up his benefits under the policy, he may use his asset protection benefit toward an annuity. He and his spouse are exempt from the requirement of naming the state as remainder beneficiary of the annuity if the annuity is a countable resource. If the annuity is not a countable resource (because it is a qualified annuity in payout status), he and his spouse are not exempt from Medicaid's annuity requirements regarding naming the state as beneficiary. 09 OHIP/ADM-3, at 12; GIS 07 MA/020, at 2; Medicaid Reference Guide, at 433.

If the State is not named as beneficiary, the purchase of the annuity may be treated as an uncompensated transfer of assets, which will be subject to a penalty period. If some of the Dollar for Dollar disregard is not needed to establish resource eligibility, it may be used to offset the amount of the transfer. GIS 07 MA/020, at 2; 09 OHIP/ADM-3, at 12; Medicaid Reference Guide, at 433.

THE "NURSING HOME WITHOUT WALLS" PROGRAM

New York's Long Term Home Health Care Program (LTHHCP) is also known as the "Nursing Home Without Walls Program." Sometimes it is referred to as "the Lombardi Program," after Tarky Lombardi, the New York State Senator who championed the health care bill which made the program possible.

States can use Medicaid money to pay for long-term care for people in nursing homes. Section 1915(c) of the federal Social Security Act lets States ask the federal Center for Medicare and Medicaid Services for a special waiver which will let the State use Medicaid money to pay for long-term care for people at home. 42 U.S.C. section 1396n (c). Waivers are good for five years. 11 OLTC/ADM-1, at 2.

New York State applied for and received a 1915(c) waiver from the federal government to run the Lombardi program. The current waiver is in effect from September 1, 2010 through August 31, 2015. 11 OLTC/ADM-1, at 2.

A person can participate in the Lombardi program if he could go into a nursing home, but would prefer to remain at home. Normally, if he remained at home, the community Medicaid rules would apply. Under community Medicaid, the resource limit for a community spouse is lower than the resource limit for a community spouse whose husband is in a nursing home. Under the Lombardi program, a community spouse can keep the same amount of resources as a community spouse whose husband is in a nursing home; she is not limited to the community Medicaid rule. 11 OLTC/ADM-1, at 14.

INTENDED RECIPIENTS:

If a person is medically eligible for placement in a nursing home but would prefer to receive services at home, or in the home of a responsible adult, or in an Adult Care Facility, Medicaid might pay for his services through this program. N.Y. Social Services Law section 367-c (2) and (5); N.Y. Public Health Law section 3616 (1); 18 NYCRR 505.21 (a)(1); Medicaid Reference Guide, at 729.

GOALS OF THE PROGRAM:

The program was designed to prevent people from being institutionalized prematurely, to let people return to the community after they have been institutionalized, and to cut costs. Long Term Home Health Care Program Reference Manual, page 1-2.

DOCTOR DETERMINATION:

If a person's doctor determines that the person could safely remain in his own home or the home of a responsible adult or an Adult Care Facility if the necessary services were provided, then the person can be assessed for the Lombardi program. 18 NYCRR 505.21 (b)(2); GIS 08 OLTC/008. If the doctor determines that the person cannot be cared for safely there, the person cannot be admitted into the Lombardi program. Long Term Home Health Care Program Reference Manual, at 1-3.

ASSESSMENT:

There will be a comprehensive assessment of the applicant's medical, social and environmental needs. N.Y. Public Health Law section 3616 (1); Medicaid Reference Guide, at 730.

If the applicant is in a hospital or residential health care facility, the assessment shall be performed by persons designated by the Commissioner, including the applicant's physician, the hospital/residential health care facility's discharge coordinator, a representative of the local department of social services, and a representative of the agency which will provide the services to the applicant. N.Y. Public Health Law section 3616 (1); 18 NYCRR 505.21 (b)(2)(i).

If the applicant is at home, the assessment shall be performed by persons designated by the Commissioner, including the applicant's physician, a representative of the local Department of Social Services, and a representative of the agency which will provide the services to the applicant. N.Y. Public Health Law section 3616 (1); 18 NYCRR 505.21 (b)(2)(ii).

If the applicant is in an Adult Care Facility, the assessment shall be performed by representatives of the Lombardi program and the local Department of Social Services, in consultation with the operator of the Adult Care Facility. 18 NYCRR 505.21 (b)(2)(iv).

A registered nurse must complete the New York State Long Term Care Placement Form Medical Assessment Abstract (DMS-1 form) to determine medical eligibility. The form records medical status, nursing care needs, incontinence, functional status, mental impairments, and rehabilitation therapy needs. Long Term Home Health Care Program Reference Manual, at 2-3. The form may be found in the manual.

A person must have a DMS-1 score of 60 or greater to qualify for the program. GIS 08 OLTC/008; Long Term Home Health Care Program Reference Manual, at 1-3.

The New York State Health Department Numerical Standards Master Sheet is used for scoring. Instructions are found in the New York State Department of Health Guidelines for Completing the Long Term Care Placement Form Medical Assessment Abstract (DMS-1). Long Term Home Health Care Program Reference Manual, at 2-3. The master sheet and guidelines may be found in the manual. If a person's score isn't high enough, and it does not accurately reflect the care he needs, his doctor may provide a written override. Long Term Home Health Care Program Reference Manual, at 2-3 to 2-4.

The Home Assessment Abstract (DSS 3139) is used to determine how the person's needs can be met at home. Long Term Home Health Care Program Reference Manual, at 2-6. This form may be found in the manual.

The initial assessment shall serve as the basis for the development and provision of an appropriate Plan of Care. N.Y. Public Health Law section 3616 (1); 18 NYCRR 505.21 (b)(2). Two other documents are created based on the initial assessment: a Summary of Service Requirements and a Proposed Monthly Budget. Long Term Home Health Care Program Reference Manual, at 2-22.

See 11 OLTC/ADM-1, Attachment III for a description of the division of responsibilities between the Department of Social Services and the Lombardi agency.

Note that the person must need case management and at least one other waiver service every thirty days in order to qualify for the program. 11 OLTC/ADM-1, at 11.

REASSESSMENT:

If a person is accepted into the Lombardi program, his medical, social and environmental needs shall be reassessed at least every 180 days. N.Y. Public Health Law section 3616 (2); 11 OLTC/ADM-1, at 5. Note that 18 NYCRR 505.2.1 (b)(8)(i) has not been updated to reflect the change from 120 to 180 days.

He is reassessed using the DMS-1 and the Home Assessment Abstract, and his doctor must verify that he can still be cared for at home. Long Term Home Health Care Program Reference Manual, at 2-21.

The agency's registered professional nurse or professional therapist must supervise the person providing personal care services by visiting the home at least every 120 days. 18 NCYRR 505.21 (c)(3) and (4).

If the agency providing the services believes that the person's level of care has changed between assessments periods, the agency must notify the social services district and a new assessment must be authorized. 18 NYCRR 505.21 (b)(8)(ii).

CAP ON COST OF CARE AT HOME:

If the person is at home, there is a cap on the total cost of Medicaid services which can be provided under this program. The monthly expenditures cannot exceed 75% of the average Medicaid cost for comparable nursing home care in that region. N.Y. Social Services Law section 367-c (2) and (3); 18 NYCRR 505.21 (b)(4)(i)(b). In other words, if caring for the person at home would cost more than caring for him in a nursing home, he would not qualify for the Lombardi program.

If the person is at home and the budget shows that his care will cost less than the 75% cap: he can get credit for the amount under the cap. The Social Services District may authorize him to use that credit during the next twelve months to get services over the cap. 18 NYCRR 505.21 (b)(4)(i)(c).

If the person is at home and the budget shows that his care will cost less than 75% of the cap: the provider can give additional services which would cost less than 10% of the monthly total, up to the 75% cap, without prior approval of the Social Services District. 18 NYCRR 505.21 (b)(4)(i)(d).

The Social Services official can authorize payment of more than the cap for a particular month if it can be reasonably anticipated that the total for the year will not exceed the cap. N.Y. Social Services Law section 367-c (2) and (3); 18 NYCRR 505.21 (b)(4)(i)(e).

If two people in the same household would qualify for the program, services can be provided which do not exceed the combined 75% budget cap for both people. They get a combined budget rather than a separate budget for each person. If the cost of their care is under the 75% cap, they can get credit for the amount under the cap. 18 NYCRR 505.21(b)(4)(i)(b) & (c); Long Term Home Health Care Program Reference Manual, at 4-12.

PEOPLE WITH SPECIAL NEEDS:

If a person has "special needs," the Social Services District may authorize up to 100% of the average Medicaid cost for comparable nursing home care in that district. N.Y. Social Services Law section 367-c (3-a)(a); 18 NYCRR 505.21 (b)(5). If a person has special needs and he has spent less than the cap, he can get credit for the amount under the cap. If reassessment shows that he needs additional services, the Social Services District may authorize him to use that credit during the next 12 months. 18 NYCRR 505.21 (b)(5).

If a person has special needs, the Social Services official can authorize payment of more than the cap for a particular month if it can be reasonably anticipated that the total for the year will not exceed the cap. 18 NYCRR 505.21 (b)(5).

"Special needs" includes people who need respiratory therapy, tube feeding, decubitus care or insulin therapy which cannot be appropriately provided by a personal care aide. It also includes people who have a mental disability as defined in Mental Hygiene Law section 1.0.3 or AIDS or dementia, including Alzheimer's Disease. N.Y. Social Services Law section 367-c (3-a)(b); 18 NYCRR 505.21 (b)(5)(i)(a); 18 NYCRR 505.21(b)(5)(i)(b).

New York Mental Hygiene Law section 1.03 (3) states, "'Mental disability' means mental illness, mental retardation, developmental disability, alcoholism, substance dependence or chemical dependence."

The number of people who get care under the Special Needs rule is limited to 25% of the total number of people getting care under the Lombardi Program within that social services district. However, if a district contains a city with a population of one million or more, the limit shall be 15%. Social Services Law section 367-c (3-a)(c); 18 NYCRR 505.21 (b)(5)(ii). If a social services district reaches that limit, it needs approval from the commissioner to authorize payment to additional people with Special Needs. 18 NYCRR 505.21 (b)(5)(iii).

CAP ON COST OF CARE IN AN ADULT CARE FACILITY:

If the person in an Adult Care Facility, there is a cap on the total cost of Medicaid services which can be provided under this program. The monthly expenditures cannot exceed 50% of the average monthly rates paid for nursing home services in that social services district. N.Y. Social Services Law section 367-c (5); 18 NYCRR 505.21 (b)(4)(ii)(b). The cap is 50% rather than 75% because many services which would be required at home are provided by staff at the Adult Care Facility. The 50% cap applies only to services provided by the long term home health care provider; it does not include services which are the responsibility of the Adult Care Facility. Long Term Home Health Care Program Reference Manual, at 7-6. The manual contains a chart on pages 7-8 through 7-9 showing which services are the responsibility of the Adult Care Facility and which are the responsibility of the long term home health care provider.

If the person is in an Adult Care Facility and the budget shows that his care will cost less than the 50% cap: he can get credit for the amount under the cap. The Social Services District may authorize him to use that credit during the next twelve months to get additional services up to the cap. N.Y. Social Services Law section 367-c(5); 18 NYCRR 505.21 (b)(4)(ii)(c).

If the person is in an Adult Care Facility and the budget shows that his care will cost less than 50% of the cap: the provider can give additional services which would cost less than 10% of the monthly total, up to the 50% cap, without prior approval of the Social Services District. 18 NYCRR 505.21 (b)(4)(ii)(d).

The Social Services official can authorize payment of more than the cap for a particular month if it can be reasonably anticipated that the total for the year will not exceed the cap. N.Y. Social Services Law section 367-c (5); 18 NYCRR 505.21 (b)(4)(ii)(e).

APPLICANT'S RESOURCE ELIGIBILITY:

The applicant can keep $13,800 in resources. GIS 10 MA/026, at 2.

APPLICANT'S INCOME ELIGIBILITY:

The applicant can keep $350 per month of his income. This is shown as "Personal Needs Allowance for Certain Waiver Participants Subject to Spousal Impoverishment Budgeting" in GIS 10 MA/026, at 2. Note that this is more than the $50 per month of income he would be allowed to keep if he were in a nursing home.

06 OMM/ADM-3, at 3 states that in accordance with Evans v. Wing and De Buono, 277 A.D.2d 903 (2000) the Personal Needs Allowance (PNA) for a person living in the community who meets the definition of "institutionalized spouse" must be higher than the PNA for a person in a

nursing home. Evans v. Wing explains that prior to 01/01/1995, the PNA for someone in the Lombardi program, whether or not he had a community spouse, was the amount of the Medicaid Needs Allowance for a one-person household in the community. The state tried to change that so that PNA would be the same as the PNA for a person in a nursing home. The court found that the new rule was irrational because it treated dissimilar financial situations equally. A person in a nursing home has fewer out of pocket expenses because his room and board are paid for by Medicaid. The court mentioned, but did not cite, Health Care Financing Administration opinion letters which reasoned that the personal needs of a person receiving home and community-based services includes the cost of food, shelter and clothing. The court concluded that the $50 PNA rule was inappropriate, but so was the pre-1995 rule. The old rule failed to take into consideration that the financial needs of a Lombardi participant living with a spouse are different from the financial needs of a Lombardi participant living alone. The cost of increasing a household from one person to two persons is less than the cost of maintaining a household for one person.

COMMUNITY SPOUSE'S RESOURCE RULE:

If the applicant is age 65 or older, the "Spousal Impoverishment Rules" apply. The community spouse resource rule is the same as if the applicant were in a nursing home. GIS 07 MA/018.

COMMUNITY SPOUSE'S INCOME RULE:

If the applicant is age 65 or older, the community spouse income rule is the same as if the applicant were in a nursing home. GIS 07 MA/018.

LOOKBACK PERIOD:

If someone applies for the Lombardi program, he only needs to provide proof of the current value of his resources. There is no lookback period. GIS 07 MA/018; 04 OMM/ADM-6, Attachment I under "Community Coverage With Community-Based Long-Term Care."

TRANSFERS & PENALTY PERIODS:

If someone applies for the Lombardi program and he made transfers, there is no penalty period. GIS 07 MA/018. Please note that GIS 07 MA/018 was issued on September 24, 2007. When reading any articles, keep this date in mind; the article may have been written before this GIS was issued. The Long Term Home Health Care Program Reference Manual appears to have been written before this GIS was issued.

ANNUITIES:

There are certain requirements for annuities purchased on or after 02/08/2006. They are discussed elsewhere in this book. Those requirements do not apply to applicants of the Lombardi program. GIS 07 MA/018; Medicaid Reference Guide, at 452.

SERVICES ALLOWED BY THE FEDERAL WAIVER:

The waiver may provide services including case management services, homemaker/home health aide services and personal care services, adult day health services, habilitation services, respite care, and other services requested by the State. 42 U.S.C. section 1396n (c) (4) (B).

"Habilitation services" means services designed to assist people in acquiring, retaining, and improving the self-help, socialization and adaptive skills necessary to reside successfully in home and community based settings. 42 U.S.C. section 1396n (c)(5).

SERVICES ALLOWED UNDER THE NEW YORK STATE PROGRAM:

The regs state that a long term home health care program must provide services which shall include at a minimum: nursing services; home health aide services; medical supplies, equipment and appliances; physical therapy; occupational therapy; respiratory therapy; speech-language pathology; audiology; medical social work; nutritional services; personal care; homemaker and housekeeper services. 10

NYCRR 763.3 (a)(2).

The Administrative Directive from the Commissioners of Social Services states that a long term home health care program must provide the following services: nursing, home health aide services, physical therapy, speech therapy, occupational therapy and personal care services, including homemaker and housekeeper. In addition, it may provide eleven waivered services: home maintenance tasks, home improvement services, respite care, social day care, social transportation, home delivered meals, moving assistance, personal emergency response services, respiratory therapy, nutritional counseling and education, and medical social services. 92 ADM-15, at 6.

The 2010 waiver changed "Home Improvement Services" to "Environmental Modifications." See 11 OLTC/ADM-1, at 8-10 and Attachment II for requirements.

The 2010 waiver added Community Transition Services, which is one-time assistance with the cost of moving expenses and/or establishing a household when transitioning from a nursing facility to the community. See 11 OLTC/ADM-1, at 10 and Attachment II, which provide examples.

The 2010 waiver added Assistive Technology, which includes Personal Emergency Response Systems and newer technology. See 11 OLTC/ADM-1, at 10-11 and Attachment II, which provide examples.

The 2010 waiver added Home and Community Support Services. It combines personal care with oversight and supervision and cueing services, as well as assistance with the activities of daily living and/or instrumental activities of daily living for people who have cognitive defects and need supervision and safety monitoring. See 11 OLTC/ADM-1, at 11 and Attachment II.

"Home care services" is defined in N.Y. Public Health Law section 3602 (1) as those services provided by a home care services agency; home health aide services; personal care services; homemaker services; housekeeper or chore services.

"Home health aide services" is defined in N.Y. Public Health Law section 3602(4) as simple health care tasks, personal hygiene services, housekeeping tasks essential to the patient's health and other related supportive services.

"Personal care services" is defined in N.Y. Public Health Law section 3602 (5) as services to assist with personal hygiene, dressing, feeding and household tasks essential to the patient's health.

"Homemaker services" is defined in N.Y. Public Health Law section 3602 (6) as assistance and instruction in managing and maintaining a household, dressing, feeding, and incidental household tasks.

"Housekeeper services" is defined in N.Y. Public Health Law section 3602 (7) as light work or household tasks which do not require the services of a trained homemaker.

See 11 OLTC/ADM-1, Attachment II for descriptions of some of the other waiver services.

LOMBARDI PROVIDERS:

To find Lombardi providers, go to:
www.homecare.nyhealth.gov
You will see a map. Click on the appropriate county.
Then click on Long-Term Home Health Care Program.

LONG-TERM HOME HEALTH CARE REFERENCE MANUAL

Note that 11 OLTC/ADM-1, at 3, dated April 27, 2011, states that the Long Term Home Health Care Reference Manual is under revision.

SAMPLE SPOUSAL REFUSAL LETTER

[spouse's address]
[date]

[Name and address of person at
county Department of Social Services
who receives Medicaid applications
for people in nursing homes]

Re: John Smith -- Medicaid Application

Dear _____:

My spouse, John Smith, is at Best Ever Nursing Home. He is applying for Medicaid.

I refuse to contribute my resources and income to pay for my spouse's medical costs, including his nursing home room and board. I understand that under New York Social Services Law section 366 (3), his Medicaid eligibility must be determined solely on the basis of his own income and resources, now that you have been informed that I will not be contributing to his medical costs.

Sincerely,

Mary Smith

FINDING DOCUMENTS AND INFORMATION ONLINE

Many of the sources mentioned in this book can be found online. Care should be taken to determine whether the online document is official or unofficial, and when it was last updated.

18 NYCRRR and 10 NYCRR:
www.dos.state.ny.us
A-Z Index
Rules and Regulations
Administrative Rules Home
NYCRR: Official Compilation of Codes, Rules and Regulations of the State of New York
View the Unofficial NYCRR Online Here

New York Laws, such as Social Services Law; Estates, Powers and Trusts Law; Public Health Law; Mental Hygiene Law:
www.assembly.state.ny.us
Bill Search & Legislative Information
New York State Laws

Or: www.senate.state.ny.us
Legislation
Click Here To View The Laws Of New York

Medicaid Reference Guide:
www.health.state.ny.us
A-Z Index
M
Medicaid
Reference Guides
Medicaid Reference Guide (MRG)

Administrative Directives (ADMs), Informational Letters (INFs), GIS
Messages, Local Commissioner Memorandum and Fair Hearings:
www.wnylc.net
Welfare Law
NYS Agency Materials
Online Resource Center
Agency Directives
     For fair hearings, you need to create a user name and password.
Once you have logged in with your user name and password, you will
see FAIR HEARINGS on the left side of the screen. Note that fair
hearings only appear if someone chose to post them.

Or: www.health.state.ny.us
A-Z INDEX
M
Medicaid
Reference Guides
Library of Official Documents

U.S.C.:
www.law.cornell.edu
U.S. Code

Internal Revenue Code:
U.S.C. Title 26

Social Security Act:
U.S.C. Title 42, Chapter 7

HCFA Transmittal 64:
www.cms.hhs.gov
Regulations and Guidance
Under Guidance: click on Manuals
Paper-Based Manuals
Scroll down to the bottom of the screen and click on Next
45 The State Medicaid Manual
Chapter 3 -- Eligibility
sm 03 3 325 to 3259.8

CFR:
www.archives.gov
Federal Register
Code of Federal Regulations (CFR)

The Long-Term Home Health Care Program Manual: A Guide for Local District Staff and LTHHCP Providers:
www.health.state.ny.us
A-Z Index
M
Medicaid
Reference Guides
Long-Term Home Health Care Program Reference Manual

The Deficit Reduction Act of 2005:
www.thomas.gov
Under Search Bill Summary and Status, click on Try The Advanced Search
Under Select Congress, click on 109
Under Enter Search, type S.1932 then click on search
Scroll down until you can click on S.1932
Text of legislation

INDEX

Made in the USA
Lexington, KY
16 October 2014